Dedicated to the memory of my Mum,
Freda Goodwin 1921–2007

RAY GOODWIN
CANOEING

Cover photograph: Lina Patel.

First published in Great Britain 2011 by Pesda Press

Unit 22, Galeri

Doc Victoria

Caernarfon

Gwynedd

LL55 1SQ

ISBN: 78-1-906095-26-0

Printed in China. www.latitudepress.co.uk

Contents

Thanks and acknowledgements

Geoff Warren introduced me to the world of the outdoors when I joined the Venture Scouts. I climbed my first mountains and paddled my first rivers under Geoff's leadership. With good friends Steve Palmer and Tony George, I had many fine adventures on the hills and rocks of Britain and further afield. In my 30s, Bob Llewellyn introduced me to the adventure of kayaking rivers and the sea. That continued with Roger Ward and then Loel Collins with the latter introducing me to the canoe.

Coaches I have worked with or have been coached by have influenced me greatly, notably Robert Egelstaff, Loel Collins, Martin Dutton, Franco Ferrero, Colin Broadway, Leo Hoare, Nigel Garrett and Dave Luke.

From North America I would thank the following: Harry Rock, Mike Cichanowski of We No Nah and the inimitable Cliff Jacobson.

Numerous people have been behind my camera when the opportunities for good photos arose but special thanks are due to Lina Patel, Bob Timms, Dave Luke and Steve Chaplin.

A chance meeting with Stuart Bell left me inspired to carry out many adventurous journeys in Scotland. Some trips have been instrumental in forming, challenging or confirming ideas and I thank the following for sharing them with me: Andy Hall, Martin Dutton, Alun Pugh, Jamie Ellson, Tim Bird, Graham Rowe, Dave Howie, Chris Charlton, Tony Howard and Mike Hazelhurst. Special thanks are due to Rob Egelstaff for sharing his concept of a canoe circumnavigation of Wales.

Ray Mears enriched the manner in which I interact with the boreal forest.

Thanks also to PGL staff for assistance and hospitality and the staff of Gwersyll yr Glan-Llyn, a Welsh-speaking outdoor centre on the shores of Llyn Tegid. 'Diolch yn fawr' for all the support over the years.

Huw Evans and Whitewater Consultancy supported me with Mad River Canoes for many years. Huw died far too young and I will miss his grin at the production of this book. Richard Bennett of Outdoor Active now supports me with We No Nah Canoes.

Jen Somogyi gave me confidence to write in my own style. Having seen my pain while writing articles, she always swore she would leave me if I wrote a book. We parted many years ago but have remained friends; she would not have been disappointed in the angst and dithering.

A big thank you goes to all my customers from the absolute beginners to people that should be considered experts in their own right. The questions you have asked, the way you look at things so differently and the expertise you have shared have all contributed to my knowledge.

Julian Fulbrook looked over my work with a critical eye coupled with support and enthusiasm. I have taken some of his ideas onboard and the book is richer for that.

Finally, I would like to say an especially big thank you to my partner Lina Patel who has had to tolerate four years of this project. She assures me that if I think of writing a second book she will …

Ray has paddled extensively in Europe and his British canoe trips include the Circumnavigation of Wales and the Irish Sea Crossing. In North America he has canoed the Rio Grande in the South and paddled as far north as the Arctic Circle, as well as doing two kayak descents of the Grand Canyon. In addition to being a British Canoe Union Level 5 Coach in Canoe, Inland and Sea Kayak, he holds a Mountain Instructor's Certificate and has led ice climbs on Kilimanjaro, Mount Kenya and in the Atlas Mountains.

He runs his own coaching and guiding business.

www.raygoodwin.com

Introduction

This is a book that is primarily about canoeing techniques; the aim is to suggest ways in which they can be applied skilfully. Just as with canoe design, so canoe techniques can have infinite variety and adaptation. The theory is useful, but even more important is the application of the right technique at the right time in the right place. As a canoe coach I have tried to teach not just the essential technical points, but also the judgment necessary to know when to put those methods into practice. Some of this judgment comes with personal experience, which often has to be acquired 'the hard way'. But, as one of Oscar Wilde's characters points out, 'Experience is the name everyone gives to their mistakes'. However, it is useful to learn from the experience of others rather than have to find out everything for yourself.

In canoeing, the leading text for the last 30 years has been the excellent *Path of the Paddle: An Illustrated Guide to the Art of Canoeing*, first published in Canada by the incomparable Bill Mason in 1980. Although updated by his son in 1995 and supplemented considerably by Paul Mason's collaboration with Mark Scriver on *Thrill of the Paddle* in 1999, there comes a point when there is a need for a fresh approach. Although Bill Mason was a superlative film-maker and photographer, printing and publishing have moved forward and some of the black and white photography of *Path of the Paddle* looks increasingly dated. Gary and Joanie McGuffin took the Bill Mason format and, with the help of excellent photography and colour printing, produced *Paddle Your Own Canoe*. Although the McGuffin manual is a visually stunning book, it deals with only a relatively narrow range of canoeing techniques. The masterly Cliff Jacobson has produced a series of books on a wide range of canoe topics, including his excellent *Expedition Canoeing*, but does not attempt to deal extensively with technique. Bill Mason of course always happily acknowledged that he was an author 'who believes there is no such thing as the last word or the last photograph on the subject of canoeing'. My attempts therefore to 'see a little further' is most definitely by 'standing on the shoulders of giants'.

By introducing some of the latest canoeing performance skills, based on what I have discovered through decades of coaching and guiding, I hope to inspire a new generation of paddlers. In particular I hope to show you, through the use of photographs acquired over many years of paddling around the world, some glimpses of the reality of canoeing: sometimes gritty, but always enthralling.

For Iain

Happy Paddling

Cartoon by Bill Bentall.

Early morning on Bark Lake on the Mississagi.

The Traditional Canoe

'The convenience of these canoes is great in these streams, full of cataracts or waterfalls and rapids through which it is impossible to take any boat. When you reach them, you load canoe and baggage upon your shoulders and go overland until the navigation is good; and then you put your canoe back into the water, and embark again.'

René Bréhant de Galinée c. 1670 French missionary and explorer.

For me the canoe means many things.

It is a craft of great beauty and practicality. There is a beauty in the way the canoe fits into a landscape. It connects us to water and the environment with an intimacy that can be so lacking in other aspects of our lives.

Many times I have paddled at night; as the sun sets the darkness heightens our senses. I have slid across stars reflected in the still black bottomless dark of a lake; a dark so deep that I have not seen the join between water and land. On other occasions I have been glad to be ashore and out of the gathering storm.

I have danced on moving water and known what it is to be at one with the movement of canoe and current. Handled well, the canoe takes on a life of its own and shows a willingness to do the moves. But there are times when the niceties go and it comes down to the adrenalin-fuelled rush of whitewater.

For me, tandem paddling is a great pleasure: a coordination of two people's effort. Canoeing is a dance which can be so much better performed with a partner. Understanding needs to be shared to allow perfect control. With time, we end up effortlessly reading each other's minds and body movements. At its best, it is a beautiful ballet.

Origins

Wherever humans have had access to large trees and a desire to travel on water, the canoe has been a ubiquitous solution. **Dugout canoes** were used all over the world and ancient examples have been found in lake and river sediments. In the Pacific they formed the basis of the greatest seaborne migrations of all time with every island having its settlers long before the Europeans 'discovered' them. The means for this settlement was the dugout, whether single or twin-hulled or with outriggers.

Across the hard rocks of Canada's Precambrian Shield the landscape was scoured by ice sheets some 20,000 years ago. When the ice finally retreated, the lakes, marshes and rivers filled the hollows. The boreal forest covered everything else. The most effective way to travel in summer was by linking the waterways. This required a boat that could be portaged. Around the world and in North America various barks had been used to make canoes, but most lack flexibility and are inclined to split along its length. With **birch bark** the grain runs around the trunk so it flexes this way without splitting. Freed of the restrictions of the dugout, canoe builders could suit shape to purpose.

The word *canoe* appears to owe its origin to one of the now-extinct Caribbean languages. The Spanish brought that name back to Europe.

Tana River, Kenya, in a dugout canoe.

Pictograph in the Woodland Caribou Park of Ontario.

Canoe Manned by Voyageurs Passing a Waterfall. These were the 'trucks' of the Canadian fur trade. The painting is by Francis Anne Hopkins and that is her sitting in the middle alongside her husband. *National Archives of Canada (1989-401-1X; C27710).*

Birch bark canoe built by Ray Mears and Pinnock Smith using traditional tools. Photo courtesy of Ray Mears.

Canoe terminology.

Boat Design

Canoes are used from the tropics to the sub-Arctic. They are made in many different materials and used for a variety of purposes. It is a small wonder that many different designs have evolved. In order to choose the right boat for the job, we need to know a little about canoe design.

If our canoe is designed to turn it needs a degree of **rocker**. This is the way the hull turns up at the end so the under-surface acts a little like a rocking chair. The freer the ends the easier it will turn but, conversely, the more correction it will need for straight running. We can increase the rocker of many traditional canoes by putting them on their edge.

The **entry line** of the canoe will affect the speed and dryness of a boat. In the photo above, the middle canoe has a sharp entry and the sides are slab-like so the hull tracks better and is more efficient on flat water. On big waves, however, the bow will cut in and ship more water. The left canoe has a blunt entry and the bow gains width quickly. From the waterline the hull flares outwards. These features make it a very dry boat in whitewater. Volume and lift are engaged quickly and waves are turned outwards. Third from the left is a Prospector, a classic does-it-all design. In both cases the hulls are **symmetric** allowing them to be paddled in either direction. On the right is a We No Nah Jensen 18. The hull is **asymmetric** and is designed to go in one direction only. The entry is sharp and the whole boat designed for speed and ease of travel.

The cross section will determine a canoes stability and manoeuvrability (coupled with rocker). **Initial stability** is how stable a canoe feels when flat on calm water. **Secondary stability** is how stable it is when leant either for ease of paddling or on waves.

| flat bottom | shallow arch | shallow V | round bottom |

We No Nah Jenson 18.

Some cheaper boats are designed with flat bottoms and are often wide as well. Initially very stable, when leant they pass a critical point and there is an abrupt change to instability. The classic canoe shape is a shallow arch. This design gives good initial and secondary stability. It is a responsive hull shape. A shallow v can work well but in some designs the point of the V ends with a 'keel' running the length of the canoe. If it has a keel this becomes a real wear point on plastic canoes and can snag on rocks. A round bottom is really only found on flat water race boats. It has little stability but is used to maximise race speed.

Bell Northwind.

The Bell Northwind is fast touring canoe constructed from carbon-kevlar. Most who paddle such thoroughbred boats will use lightweight bent paddles and use 'sit and switch'. In the mid-section, **tumblehome** is apparent. This is the inward curve of the hull before it meets the gunwale. It gives greater strength to the hull and enables you to stroke close to the hull without hitting the gunwale.

Mark Maier puts a solo canoe through a classic flat-water freestyle move. Often choreographed to music, freestyle has the grace and finesse of ballet.

True solo canoes tend to be much narrower and are faster for the lone paddler. In the UK most people paddle small tandem boats as solo canoes. This seems to suit what we do, but it is a joy to get into a performance boat.

Flat-water race canoes can get very narrow and, with their rounded hulls (designed to minimise wetted surface area and maximise speed), will be impossibly unstable for the majority. In the hands of an expert, however, they are incredibly fast.

Specialist whitewater canoes are shorter and have a pronounced rocker. Outfitting includes a saddle, foot pegs and thigh straps. It is not only possible to paddle big whitewater but also roll the canoe. Whereas traditional canoes are usually used on whitewater up to about grade 3, the design and outfitting of specialist whitewater canoes allows them to be used up to grade 5. Some paddlers will transfer selected elements of the outfitting into the more traditional boat for greater control in whitewater.

Freestyle open canoes have flat planing hulls, low volume ends and 'extreme' buoyancy bagging and outfitting. The paddler still kneels and all space is packed with buoyancy. This allows them to surf waves and perform the 3D acrobatics required to compete in freestyle events. Most freestyle canoes are are made by converting kayak hulls but some, such as the Spanish Fly, are designed as canoes.

Decked C1s are designed as river runners or freestyle boats. Some are designed as canoes but the majority are converted from kayak hulls. The paddler still kneels and uses a single blade but the hull is sealed with a spraydeck. This means the boat doesn't take on water and is easier to roll than an open boat.

Flat water race canoe (C1). Paddler is Chris Calvert.

Chris Noble in an Esquif Zoom. The insert shows outfitting and release toggle easily to hand. The strapping is so tight that the release must be within easy reach.

Chris Noble in a Riot Astro which started life as a kayak. The cockpit of the kayak has been cut off and a new rim welded on. Photo courtesy of Pete Catterall.

Chris Noble paddling a C1 converted from a Jackson Allstar kayak. This is very much intended as a playboat; a river runner would have more volume and length for an easier ride.

A cedar canvas canoe.

Boat Materials

Canoes are made of many materials from the traditional to the hi-tech. In the photo above, the wooden planking of the canoe has a canvas skin stretched over the outside (***cedar canvas***) which is then waterproofed. There is normally a brass running strip down the keel. These boats are aesthetically pleasing. If you can store the boat under shelter and do not intend to paddle whitewater, this is a superb boat.

A ***cedar strip*** canoe is made with much thinner strips of wood. The joints can be glued and then varnished, negating the need for the canvas skin. A variant on this is where the strips are initially fastened to an internal frame that is removed in the latter stages of construction, leaving a hull with no internal ribs. A clear fibreglass skin adds strength. These boats are aesthetically pleasing and surprisingly robust. They do require care both in storage and maintenance but they are a real attention-grabber for onlookers.

Left: a cedar strip canoe built with internal ribs to add strength. Right: a cedar strip canoe built without ribs. Photo and boats by Valerie Welch using plans supplied by Carrying Place Canoe & Boat Works Ontario.

The **aluminium** canoe was developed by Grumman, a company that produced fighter aircraft using stretch-formed aluminium. The Vice President, William Hoffman, had been on a canoe trip in 1944 and after portaging a heavy canoe realised he could make a lighter boat from aluminium. End 'tanks' contain buoyancy to keep the canoe afloat in a capsize. Aluminium canoes dominated the market for some years. They are durable and robust but also cold and noisy.

Coleman canoes are made using a plastic that is relatively soft and lacks rigidity. This is overcome by running metal tubing internally down the centre of the boat and attaching thwarts to it. Boats can be loaded into rail containers with the hulls stacked one inside the other with the final assembly completed at the destination. This cheaper transportation, coupled with quicker construction methods, means the Coleman style canoe could beat any other canoe on price.

With a double or triple-layering system, **polyethylene** canoes are rigid enough not to need internal bracing. Being honeycombed the canoe will float even when swamped, although only just. It is repairable by welding additional material in place. It is a cheaper material than Royalex but is heavier and does not have the same 'memory'.

Royalex is the plastic of choice for many whitewater paddlers. It combines rigidity and robustness with relative lightness. It also has 'memory'; if bent it will want to return to its original shape (albeit slightly creased). On the downside, it is a soft material and scratches easily. Royalex is an engineered material of multiple layers which have been bonded together. ABS middle layers are sandwiched by exterior vinyl skins that give protection against UV and some abrasion resistance. Extra thickness is added to certain areas such as the bow or mid-boat to give rigidity. These layers are bonded and sent to the canoe manufacturers as a flat sheet. At the canoe factory the sheet is heated in an oven before being vacuumed onto a mould. After cooling, the rest of the canoe trim is added.

Kevlar or a carbon-kevlar combination gives great rigidity and is very light. It tends to be used for fast touring or racing canoes. It is an expensive material but, because of this, much thought is normally given to the design and they are efficient to paddle. Kevlar canoes are a delight to portage.

For some people the convenience of an **inflatable** canoe for ease of packing and transport provides a good choice. If technique and the dance are not your objectives, an inflatable gives you access to the adventure of canoeing. Whether travelling by car or air the canoe is easily moved to new places.

Chris Noble on the River Dee. his boat is outfitted with airbags and a kneeling thwart for use in whitewater.

Outfitting your Canoe

The environment you are going to paddle in will determine how much outfitting you need to do to your canoe. Where are you going to paddle? Maybe there is no need for extra buoyancy or outfitting. For running whitewater or on a big lake, many would prefer more buoyancy. The buoyancy has to be secured into the boat. With wooden gunwales, attachments can be screwed into the wood to provide a cross-hatch of webbing to hold an air bag or block. On a vinyl gunwale, pop rivets under the gunwale can attach the same hoops.

Here an encased foam block is fastened into the end of the canoe. It weighs more than an airbag.

Attachments can be screwed into the wood.

Attachments can be pop riveted into a vinyl gunwale.

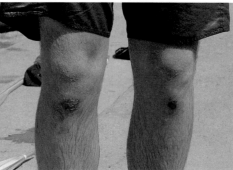

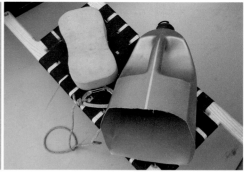

Kneeling can be hard on the knees. Wearing knee-pads (left), using a kneeling mat or gluing foam pads into the canoe will help.

Sand and grit can cause a nasty rash (right). Be meticulous in washing sand and grit from your feet and use a sponge to mop up any in your canoe.

A cut-down plastic container to use as a bailer and a sponge ensure a dry boat.

Some lace the side of a plastic canoe to make a set of totally secure attachment points (it is only terrifying with the first canoe you drill). Here the spacing on the airbag section is 3 inches and, through the centre section, 4 inches.

A piece of wood makes a template for marking the spacing; a steady application of the drill is needed to stop the bit skidding. You can put a strip of masking tape beneath the gunwale before marking to prevent this. The holes are threaded using cord (5mm climbing cord is used in the above photos).

The ends are fastened off on the inside of the canoe using overhand knots. The cord can be left plain on the inside, although leave a little slack so it can be easily used. Plastic tubing can be slotted onto the lacing cord to make clipping easy.

Having made most of the attachment points you need to think about **fastening air bags** into your canoe. The rear air bag is easy, as a simple cross lash will hold it down and the seat will prevent it moving forward. The front air bag needs a little more work to prevent it moving.

If you want to play hard then a large central air bag can be added.

A D-ring and pad are glued to the floor of the canoe. The area should be marked in pencil before being lightly sanded and cleaned. Glue needs to be used carefully and as per the instructions. Too much glue can mean a vapour will be given off that will be absorbed by (and possibly damage) the Royalex.

A strap or cord is threaded through the D-ring. The cord attached to the end of the bag is run through the interior section of the end loop and fastened off. A fastening cord is run back and forth to hold the airbag down using any eyelets on the bag. The D-ring strap is run out from under the bag and fastened to either the carrying handle or end loop.

A strong **end loop** (green) has been threaded through the canoe. Shock cord is in place to hold a **painter** or swim line. The end loop will also be the attachment point in rescuing a pinned canoe.

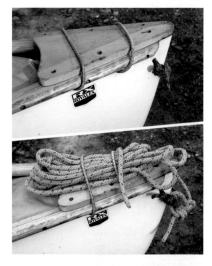

A different arrangement of the shock cords.

Traditionally, when a tandem canoe was paddled solo, the paddler faced back-to-front and used what had been the bow seat. With a load this is perfect as the canoe is well balanced in the water. With an empty canoe, the front end is still too light. Adding a **kneeling thwart** moves the paddler closer to the centre. It is important not to site it too close to the central yoke, or exiting the canoe will be difficult in a capsize. The kneeling thwart gives a remarkable amount of connection to the canoe and hence control, so many paddlers use them.

A kneeling thwart with a release mechanism built in. A small dowel pin fits into a hole in the L-section before being fastened with a quick-release strap.

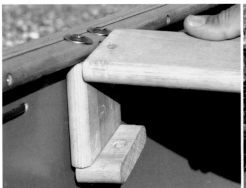

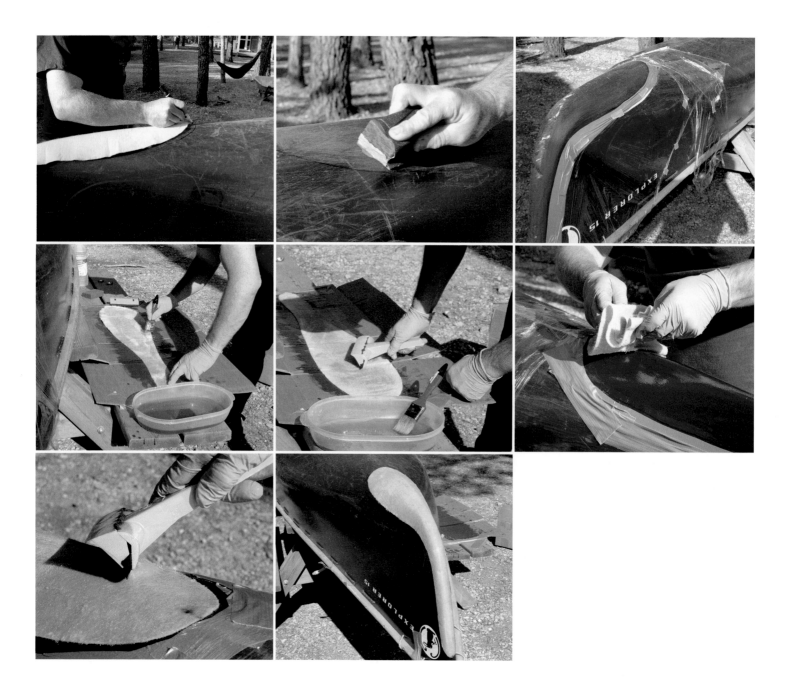

A Royalex canoe, in particular, wears at the ends of the hull. For protection you can fit a **bang plate** (also known as a skid plate). Some people will fit them from new, but since the Royalex will need sanding there seems little point. Kits are readily available with detailed instructions.

With the kevlar mat draped on the canoe, mark out the approximate area. The mat will spread further when wet. The area is lightly sanded and then cleaned. Everything surrounding the marked out area is masked and the two-part resin is thoroughly mixed.

The resin must be thoroughly pushed into the mat so a roller or squeegee is useful. The mat is spread onto the prepared canoe. Any air bubbles must be squeezed out. Once the mat is on, the canoe can be turned upright so there are no runs. Leave it to cure for a day and the job is done.

Even in the days of bark canoes some parts needed extra protection. Split spruce root has been used to fasten the gunwales to the birch bark hull. A gunwale cap has been fitted to protect the lashings. The black line is pitch used to seal a join in the bark.

Paddles

We select different paddles for a wide variety of reasons. It may be that they are suited to a particular purpose, the material they are made of, the aesthetics, feel, durability or price. Choose the wrong paddle and we make our learning and experience less satisfying or even downright frustrating.

The first three paddles from the left are whitewater paddles. They need to be robust for hitting and shoving off rocks. The first is of plastic with a metal shaft. This gives a relatively cheap paddle but there is little spring in the shaft to absorb shocks. Wooden whitewater blades can have laminated blades, but this one is strengthened with a metal tip and a covering of fibreglass matt on the blade. The third is a fusion of a metal-tipped kevlar blade on a wooden shaft. Price will have an impact on choice but, in all cases, it is important to have a clean blade face: really cheap paddles often have a reinforcing spine jutting from the centre of the blade. This breaks up the water flow and makes feeling and learning strokes harder.

The fourth blade, an Ottertail, is for deepwater only and would be easily damaged in rocky rivers. It is a great paddle to learn strokes with. With its narrow tip and the fineness of the blade it is sensitive to paddle with, easily transferring the feel of the water to the hand. Most paddlers today would consider the beavertail paddle, fifth from the left, to be a flat-water paddle. However, it was originally developed as a whitewater paddle on the high volume rivers of North America. The blade is widest near the tip, so the moment the paddle enters the water there is a positive grip. The sixth and seventh paddles are laminated flat-water paddles. They lack the robustness of a whitewater paddle, but are cheaper than the one-piece wooden paddles.

On the right is a bent-shaft paddle. It is a delight to use on journeys on flat water. It is light and efficient and makes covering a distance far easier, particularly when paddling tandem.

Choose your paddle to suit what you are doing. Do you need a robust paddle for shallows and whitewater, a sensitive paddle for aesthetics and ease of learning or a bent-shaft for efficient flat water travel? And always carry a spare to cover you in case of breakage or to collect the paddle you have dropped.

The best way of **_sizing the paddle_** with a whitewater-style blade is to stand upright and the top should be just below your chin. As a general rule it seems to work. This paddle has a T-grip that some say gives them superior grip and control in whitewater; all whitewater competition paddlers seem to use the T. Personally, I still prefer to use a palm grip for ease of switching my hand position during strokes, even in whitewater. Bent-shaft paddles need to be slightly shorter. Another method is to kneel upright on one knee and grip the throat of the paddle (the point where the blade joins the shaft). The arm should be close to horizontal or sloping down slightly. This is a good method as it measures the shaft and does not change with blade length, so can be used with most types of paddle.

For deep water, oiled rather than varnished paddles are much easier to maintain. The occasional gentle rub down with wire wool and a reapplication of oil brings them up like new.

All wooden blades are vulnerable. They need care and attention. If they are damaged on a trip, a band of gaffer tape will hold things together before a more permanent repair can be attempted. Glue and clamps may do the job but a band of fibreglass may be necessary.

These were made at a symposium where the paddle-maker was giving advice on making your own. The paddle on the right is still being carved and has the centre line drawn on the paddle shaft.

The paddle on the left has a deepwater blade. The tip is coated with resin but lacks the fibreglass sheath of its whitewater cousin. The second from the left has a whitewater blade; the wood running at right angles at the tip strengthens the laminations. There is a thin fibreglass sheet across the whole blade face adding to its robustness: a good blend of materials.

The third from the left has a strong composite blade on a wooden shaft. There is a metal insert into the tip of the blade to reduce wear. This combination makes it cheaper than the fully carbon paddle on the right.

Metal and plastic paddles are good for bashing around in shallow or rocky venues. It is important that you do not go for the cheapest option, which can have a definite raised spine running down the middle of the blade (this interferes with water flow and will slow your learning). A good combination for a beginner is one plastic blade and one really nice wooden paddle.

The appropriately dressed paddler.

Footwear & Clothing

Choosing footwear and clothing to suit the conditions is tricky, partly because there are so many options available. An old pair of trainers will do the job but, as with most footwear not specifically designed for watersports, once they are wet they will take a long time to dry. Wellies will not drag you down in the water. However, if you are kneeling a lot and in and out of the boat frequently, any water tends to first run into knees and then when you stand it drains into your boots. Walking boots are warm and solid; these are fine as long as you don't go for a swim. In this situation they are heavy and more at risk of foot entrapment (being so stiff soled).

There are many specialist alternatives. As a general principle, the more supple and comfortable the footwear the less protection it will give your feet from cold or injury. Equally, the more solid the footwear the less easy it is to kneel in the canoe and the higher the risk of your foot becoming wedged between two boulders or in a wrapped canoe.

From left to right: sandals with toe protection, water tennies, wetsuit boots and canyoning boots.

Some shoes designed to be wet will be like sandals or trainers but with the advantage of being made of materials that do not rot and are quick drying. Wetsuit boots are popular as they are cheap, warm and with a lack of bulk easy to slip out from under a seat. However, they tend to be slippery on wet grass and lack ankle support. A more substantial boot is designed for canyon scrambles. It is self-draining, with a good grip and ankle support. As long as you can fit it below your seat this is a good boot for use in rugged terrain.

Cotton clothing is pleasant on a hot day but is a disaster when it is damp or wet. It retains moisture and, when worn next to the skin, will rob the body of heat. Jeans when wet cling to the legs and strip heat away quickly. These are clothes for a nice day with something else held in reserve. For hot conditions there are many alternatives: e.g. nylon quick-drying sportswear or even mosquito- proof clothing.

For forest travel, poly-cotton trousers provide a garment with ample pockets and a resistance to fire sparks. However, though slightly better than cotton, once wet they do not function as well as fleece.

In colder conditions **undergarments** should have a 'wicking' ability. The material transfers moisture away from the skin and onto its outer face. Coupled with fleeces, a layer of air is maintained next to the body. The same effect can be achieved with natural products. For example, a shirt and a jumper of merino wool/nylon mix would keep the skin dry and build up **layers** to trap air and warmth.

A set of **waterproofs** provides the final barrier between you and the weather. They stop the rain and wind. If the material is breathable, it prevents some condensation. Paddling waterproofs may be heavy-duty with reinforced knees and bottom. Trousers can come with a waterproof sock or a latex ankle seal.

An all-in-one suit below a drysuit, which ensures no gaps in the clothing.

[1] Salopettes get rid of that uncomfortable gap that opens up between trousers and top.

[2] Sea kayaking cags make great tops for wet conditions.

Canoeists seldom use wetsuits. A wetsuit is made of tight fitting neoprene and once immersed works by trapping a layer of water between the suit and the body. They are not comfortable, but are cheap and a reasonably effective way of keeping warm if you are likely to swim. If you are going to use one, get one without arms to prevent fatigue during normal paddling. In cold windy conditions a set of waterproof trousers over the wetsuit prevents a good deal of heat loss.

A **drysuit** is the best option if you are paddling in wet cold conditions or if a swim is a distinct possibility. Latex seals at neck and wrists and further seals or dry socks at the feet keep water out. This suit is entered by a horizontal zip at the shoulders; others will have a large diagonal zip at the front. It is possible to buy drysuits with 'relief' zips; this increases the cost but is worth every penny! Another variation is that drysuits designed for sea kayaking have a built-in hood, which makes life much more comfortable in heavy rain.

Around water and rope it is a good idea to have a knife in or on your BA. I have a small folding knife tucked into a pocket; some whitewater paddlers prefer one easier to hand. A whistle is invaluable for attracting attention.

Buoyancy Aids (Personal Flotation Devices)

The **buoyancy aid** will ensure we float if out of our depth or on a whitewater river. I will maybe paddle without one on a calm day, but it is not a decision I make lightly. Even the experienced have ended up in the water without warning. BAs come in a plethora of designs. All will conform to a national standard so choice can be based on function and fit. Most manufacturers use fairly soft foam so it conforms well to the body. Foam will deteriorate over a period so it is best not to use it as a seat. Cheap versions will be simple, but most of us will want to have pockets.

Lifejackets come in various forms. This one, un-inflated, has the same floatation as most BAs. Inflated, it turns you onto your back and a collar supports your head. On the plus side, you float face up but on the minus side they make it difficult to swim; they are really designed for use by people waiting to be rescued at sea. Most people agree that lifejackets are not really suitable for canoeing.

The BA is for use by people that can swim and are in reach of rescue or the shore. It is the flotation used by most paddlers. Unlike a lifejacket, it will not keep your head above water if you are unconscious. However, it is more comfortable, warmer, provides some upper body protection from impact with rocks and allows you to swim freely in the water.

Hats and Helmets

Water will intensify the effects of the sun's rays, and so peaked or brimmed **hats**, **sunglasses** and sun cream are sensible protection. In cold conditions a warm hat is a must. If the rest of your body is efficiently clothed and waterproofed then the head is the place that loses heat. The US military did some research in the 1970s when they dressed volunteers in Arctic clothing except for their heads. The head then accounted for 40% of the heat loss. Broad-brimmed hats are really popular among canoe paddlers. Unlike the mountaineer, we are seldom out in very high winds. The brim provides shelter without compromising our side vision. However, all peaked caps can be a nightmare in woodland; while looking down to see where our feet are going, it is easy to walk into a low branch.

On whitewater, when poling and even when moving about on a slippery bank a helmet will protect your head. All canoe helmets conform to a common safety standard. They may be cut above the ears or come much lower. It is essential that the fit is good so it cannot be knocked loose. Some kayak helmets have a brim built in; this is great for a bit of shade, for those of us with glasses and keeps the rain off the face.

If you want to get ahead, get a hat.

Glasses can be secured with specialist grips. The sunglasses are designed for watersport and the securing strap is built in.

When to wear a helmet is a matter of personal choice. Paddling a kayak I would wear a helmet in all rapids. While upside down, the nearest thing to the riverbed will be your head. Meeting a rock headfirst is shocking. I have seen kayaks jump from the water with such an impact.

Capsize a traditional canoe and, if you are not strapped in, you'll end up swimming with your head on the surface instead of dangling upside down in your kayak, dragging your head along the riverbed. There are definitely times when the helmet goes on. So why are there photographs of whitewater and some of us without helmets? In every case a decision, based on experience, has been made. Safety is a way of thinking rather than a piece of gear. If you are inexperienced I would strongly advise you to wear a helmet in all rapids. Until you have done a rescue course, swum in powerful water, made your own mistakes and taken swims, you cannot make a realistic judgement. If in doubt wear one.

Keeping your Kit Dry

No system can be totally reliable so anything valuable, vulnerable or critical to your comfort should be double protected. For example, a sleeping bag would go in a dry bag within a dry sac.

Dry bags are made from a variety of materials but the principle remains the same: rolling down the top edges before clipping the rolled section seals the bag. With the addition of straps, our bag becomes a rucksack (far left) which makes portaging easier. Waterproof barrels are another way of keeping kit dry. On longer journeys, I will often carry the food in a barrel. Specialist harnesses are used for portaging.

Electronic car keys and mobile phones can be put in hard cases. These cases can go into a dry bag for further protection. Specialist dry pacs enable you to use mobile phones or radios. The phone can then be carried in a buoyancy aid pocket. Hard cases can be used to protect cameras; these are extremely reliable but do check the gaskets.

If the terrain is too rough, wheels become just another thing to carry. Rannoch Moor.

Portaging & Transport

Many hands make light work.

It was that time! We started pulling the trolley up the gravel road; this was to be a gruelling but nonetheless an essential aspect of the journey. With gritted teeth and baited breath we began. One of us was in a loop of rope five metres ahead rather like a horse pulling a cart, and the other close up next to the boat. The hauling up the gravel track was indeed brutal. Not a good sight as even in the drizzle we were stripped to the waist. Walkers passed us by with incredulous looks. Eventually we had an easier run along the concrete aqueduct to the Blackwater Reservoir, some 300m higher than our sea-level start.

A 12km paddle along the Blackwater took us into the heart of the Rannoch Moor. The trolley became just one more thing to carry in this bleak terrain broken only by peat bog and boulder. We alternated with carrying either the canoe or the enormous load of rucksack and gear. On each swap the load you took over seemed so much better than the other, but only for a brief moment!

After hours of slogging the canoe and kit in this way there was a small loch and then the railway line. Progress was much quicker with the canoe back on its trolley. In the darkness we reached the road head.

There were lights on in the hotel and people were being served. The thought of some pending refreshments was tantalising. The canoe was parked against the wall and we hurried in. The place hushed as Graham and I made our way to the bar. We were not a

Rannoch Moor portage

pretty sight after 18 hours on the go. Sweat and peat stained all our clothing and I'm sure we didn't smell of roses either. Last orders had been called and, to our dismay and shear disappointment, we were not be served.

We had not eaten for hours and were dehydrated not to mention hungry. I tried to explain to a rather tipsy landlady where we had come from, but she was frankly sceptical and unimpressed. Eventually another was dispatched to see our canoe and confirm our tale; the landlady herself then went to see just to be sure. We were now to be served.

The first pint of beer did not touch the sides and a second joined it. Then we were bought a third. In our dehydrated state this was not good. My brain appeared to function normally but was no longer connected to my mouth and sentences were beyond me. We wished all a good night, as best we could, and headed down the road to the first camp spot we could find. In the morning we would be back on the water and heading downhill. **"**

Lifting & Carrying

Lifting and carrying boats will always be an issue. However we lift, there will be a large load on the back. We need to take care to protect this vulnerable part of the body. On cold days we need to warm up before carrying boats.

With bent knees and chins up, the back is relatively straight[1]. The timing of the lift needs to be coordinated by having someone in charge. The load is to one side of the spine so it still has an impact and it is not a method that is recommended for use over a long distance.

Two people can share the load for short distances[2]. With heavy boats, this method is soon wearisome and it is hard on the back. Some prefer to carry two empty boats for a more balanced load[3].

There comes a point when it is no longer practical to carry the canoe in the hands or to use a trolley. At this point the only option is **_lifting the canoe onto the shoulders_**.

With heavier boats you should avoid lifting on your own, although you can still carry solo. Do a dummy run without actually picking up the boat so that both people are clear on the movement. Once the boat is up, one person straightens their arms supporting the canoe while the other moves under the carrying yoke. The partner, carrying gear, accompanies the carrier so we can reverse the method to put the canoe down. The partner stays with the carrier to provide warning of overhanging trees and to be at hand for the put down, which involves the same sequence in reverse. It is possible to get to the stage of being too tired to curl a boat down on your own.

Carrying the canoe in any wind is really difficult. It can be still done solo, but with a second paddler holding a bow rope to stop the canoe being blown about in the wind.

⚠ WARNING

All of the methods shown have the potential for damaging your back if done badly (or even if done well but for a prolonged distance). Ask for help or advice and know your limitations.

The carrying yoke is positioned so that the canoe can be carried in balance by one person.

Some carrying thwarts are nicely shaped and carved to fit onto the shoulder; others are just flat. For longer portages, either ready-made pads or closed cell foam and duct tape make a huge difference.

You can share the load. Those under the canoes have the seat edge across the shoulders.

Smaller paddlers should avoid lifting heavier boats on their own. If this is unavoidable, the following less strenuous method can be used with a lighter and smaller Royalex canoe. In the above photo sequence the paddler is curling the end of the canoe. Some paddlers prefer a straight lift with the canoe already upside down. They then move down the canoe until they can lower it onto their shoulders. Putting the boat down involves the same sequence in reverse.

At this point on a portage you will have already carried a load along the route so you will know the path and any obstructions. Choose a level spot for the lift. This method requires strength and good timing, but is quicker and easier if you can do it. Pull the canoe up so the edge of the hull rests on your knees. Grasp the far side of the bow seat with your left hand. Your right hand holds the central thwart near to you. With back muscles tense to protect your spine, raise the canoe up onto your knees. The back of the canoe can be left on the ground and you prepare your right knee for 'kicking' the canoe into the air. It is easier to use the powerful leg muscles to do this awkward bit of the lift. As the canoe goes up, use your arms to do the last part of the lift and then quickly step in below the boat and take the weight on your shoulders.

The next problem is ***putting the canoe down***. Slide the canoe off your shoulders and simultaneously put your right arm under it, cradling the gunwale into your elbow. Roll the canoe down onto your knees, shifting hands as you go. Allow the boat to rotate onto the ground (do not rest the end on the ground in this manoeuvre).

Kinloch Hourn to Loch Quoich. The front puller has tied a loop in the rope so that he can throw his body weight into the pull. The second person is balancing the canoe and pulling as best as possible, again with a loop of the rope.

On good surfaces it is possible to use a trolley. The canoe needs to be fastened with ropes and straps.

The Little Bear train runs from Moosonee close to the shores of James Bay. Many canoe trips finish here; there is no road, so the train company has a specialist canoe flat bed.

Transporting the Canoe

Attaching your canoe to a suitable means of transport is a skill in itself. On a small car there will be a comparatively small space between the roof bars. Car manufacturers will normally produce their own brand racks but it is often better to buy one from a specialist company.

Straps need to be tight; here they have been finished off with a series of half-hitches with the end of the strap[1].

A 'tie down' is needed at the front and back of the car[2]. The rope is inserted into the towing ring[3]. The front is tied down with small but strong rope[4]. The canoe overhangs the windscreen, and there is going to be a tremendous updraft on it. Canoes and roof racks have been torn from vehicles. Your boat could be destroyed but, far worse, it could hit a vehicle travelling behind. For long journeys it is worth removing air bags to prevent wear from flapping.

Floatplanes are covered by regulations but can often carry one or more canoes strapped to the float struts.

It is possible to put two canoes on some roofs. Note that straps run through the level canoe's straps to fasten the angled canoe. In this instance, straps rather than rope fasten front and back.

Getting canoes onto high roofs can be done from a shoulder carry. Dave slides his canoe on; he has a small stepladder for reaching straps.

In this system the canoe is strapped while the rack is at the side. Once up, the rack is locked into position.

If there is room you can use ropes to create a slide to take boats up or down from trailers. Otherwise, you may need to see-saw the top boats down from the top levels until you can lift them off.

Maya Rose Goodwin: starting young.

Getting Started

Robert and David, my two very young nephews, played in my canoe on dry land. For two imaginative days the boat voyaged to the farthest reaches of my lawn, taking in Africa and Australia on the way. On the third day I had the time to take them to the water. I tied a rope to the stern and allowed them the freedom of a rope length in a knee-deep creek. The canoe spun in circles but they never noticed in the intensity of their concentration and play. They were far too young to learn anything other than boats are fun … but what a lesson!

I have introduced so many people to canoeing, invariably on flat water. However, my own start was a little more robust. We were paddling a lot in kayaks and the canoe was seen as just a bit of fun in less serious water. Loel and I set out for the River Mawddach in a borrowed canoe. Other than the inherent buoyancy of the plastic, there was no additional buoyancy. Loel was in the stern and I, a kayaker with no idea, took the bow.

Shooting out of one set of narrows we took a set of large standing waves straight on. The first was exhilarating as I was pitched skywards, but the reckoning was approaching fast. I plunged back down and straight into the heart of the second wave. The bow disappeared and kept going down. As I surfaced Loel was shouting 'stay with it'.

'Stay with what?' I was bobbing on the surface and my end of the canoe had disappeared from beneath me. The whole situation was ludicrous and I started laughing (so

much that it hurt). The canoe eventually reappeared and we swam it to the side with no harm done. **"**

Mine was not the introduction I would recommend for most, but it was safe because of our understanding of water and the consequences of a swim … if not the boat. It was only later that I learnt the control and finesse of technique necessary in the canoe. As my experience grew, I came to love the dance that is possible both on flat and whitewater.

Trim & Positioning

Understanding how you position yourself in a canoe and move about in it are critical skills. Trim is the balance of the canoe from end to end and is fundamental. For most things we need a bow-light boat. This is achieved by thinking about which paddler is on the front seat (normally the lighter one), and where any load is placed in the canoe.

With the heavier paddler in the stern and the bow light, the front glides up and through the water. Steering is much easier. When the positions are reversed, the canoe is bow-heavy. If the boat wavers offline by the merest degree, water will pile on one side of the bow pushing it into a turn. This is hard to correct. Avoid a bow-heavy canoe for normal forward travel. With a laden canoe, check the trim by having the canoe afloat while it is loaded or, once in, by asking another crew to look.

There are a variety of kneeling and seating positions. In the top left photo, the paddler is kneeling with her knees spaced and slightly shifted to her paddling side. This is stable and she has a number of connection points to the canoe. It is effective and recommended for your first trips. A pad or knee pads will make it more comfortable. In the top right photo, she has not swapped her hands but has swapped paddling sides on this cross-deck stroke. To facilitate this rotation to her 'off' side she has moved her knees across.

Paddling positions.

If you sit with the knees up they get in the way of paddling. An alternative is to sit slightly skewed on the seat with the feet to one side. There are a variety of positions that allow you to use the seat and still have a better connection to the canoe. Some of them are quite elegant!

If you are paddling with feet below a seat or kneeling thwart be careful with chunky footwear or even big feet. If you capsize, you need to be able to get clear of the canoe so practise in an easy place.

When paddling solo you don't want a canoe to be wildly bow-light. If the boat is not fitted with a kneeling thwart, you can paddle the canoe 'back to front' so the bow seat is used facing the opposite direction. This brings your weight more towards the centre of the boat.

When getting into the canoe what matters is transferring your weight from balanced on the land to balanced in the canoe. In the first photo, weight is still on the land foot and the hands are grasping the gunwales. (She could have her paddle in her hands and laid across the gunwales). Weight is transferred to the canoe foot and, once both feet are in, she will drop down.

With two of you it is easy for one to provide stability while the other gets in. When the first is settled and kneeling, the second can step into the canoe. Some advocate that the stern paddler should get in first, but there is no hard and fast rule and it will depend on situation and experience.

If you are a beginner choose **your first paddling venue** carefully. Look at the situation. Where will the wind take me? How cold is the water? Could I swim to the shore? Do I have spare clothing available? All of us have made mistakes and ended up in the water in easy situations. You need to think about your car keys, wallet, phone or glasses. Do not presume you will be the exception.

As you practise you will gain the ability to go in a straight line, be able to turn or straighten up the canoe and master strokes such as the J for efficiency in a straight line. From the start, practise on both sides to maintain a balance in skill and muscle development.

Could you swim to
the shore?

Facing each other using a simple draw stroke to spin the canoe on the spot.

Moving on

Learning to go in a straight line is not easy and takes time and practice. Here is an alternative start that will teach some basic but fundamental skills. You may wish to skip this and proceed onto going in a straight line.

Find yourself a nice sheltered patch of water, one in which you would be comfortable swimming to the side dragging your canoe behind you. You should not fall in if you are steady with your strokes, and particularly if you are kneeling. It is best if you face and check each other. Normally, the heavier paddler would sit in the stern. In this exercise, however, he is sitting on the bow seat facing backwards and the lighter paddler in on the stern seat. The boat is trimmed more level this way. Start with a simple draw (explained below) with the paddles on opposite sides so the canoe spins.

The position of the thumb on top of the paddle is a useful indicator and check. This thumb can be pointing down or up, inwards or outwards. The photo has been staged to make the thumb obvious; we don't paddle with the thumb stuck out.

With an end-on view of the ***draw stroke***, the body position, the pushing nature of the top arm, and the draw and clip are obvious. When you first do this have your knees spread across the canoe for stability, but still pointing to the working side.

Look where you are going and not at the paddle. Knee and chest are pointed slightly towards the paddling side. In all strokes the torso is engaged so that the arm positions are strong. The paddler reaches out with both hands and the paddle indicator thumb points backwards. With the top hand pushing outwards, the bottom hand and arm draws the blade towards the canoe. Just before the paddle touches the canoe, clip it out backwards ready for a repeat.

A simple draw stroke can be used to spin the canoe on the spot or, as illustrated here, to move the boat sideways. This 'simple' stroke is versatile and powerful. We can use it to turn, go sideways, or straighten the boat while moving at speed.

Using a **simple pry** we can do the opposite of the draw to move away from the paddle. In the photo sequence below, the paddlers are going to spin the canoe by working with the paddles on opposite sides.

Slice the paddle in from behind. The paddle shaft is close to the gunwale and the indicator thumb is up. The paddle is now vertical and alongside. The shaft is against the gunwale and your hand is holding it there. Indicator thumb points back. The paddle shaft is levered off the gunwale by pulling your top hand across the canoe. Try going sideways by working both paddles on the same side. Be careful.

A bath toy focuses the attention on a target. When you first practise a stroke you will be focused on the paddle. As soon as possible, you need to look where you are going.

By using **combined draws and prys** in different ways, we can perform different manoeuvres while keeping the paddles on opposite sides of the canoe (the more usual way to paddle your boat). Both paddlers are using a draw stroke so the canoe spins[1]. By both using a pry, they can spin in the opposite direction[2]. Lina is doing a draw and Ray a pry, so the canoe goes sideways[3]. If you are learning these combinations you can face each other to make it easier to work together. Practise all of the above on both sides.

Practise a whole series of manoeuvres without swapping hands or sides. Go sideways, change direction, spin, spin the opposite way and stop. This varied practise will ensure that you progress faster. Finally, do all of the above while both paddlers face forwards.

Tandem sweep strokes.

In a tandem canoe the pivot point is between the two paddlers. This is the point which the canoe turns around in a stationary spin. In a solo canoe, the paddler does a full sweep from bow to stern. In a tandem this is ineffective, so each paddler operates in a 90-degree arc between the end of the canoe nearest them and a point at right angles to their hips. In the above sequence, the stern paddler starts at the stern of the canoe and reverse sweeps to level with his hip. The bow paddler does a forward sweep starting at the bow and doing a quarter circle until the paddle is level with her hip.

If the stern paddler does a **_forward sweep_** and the bow paddler does a reverse, the canoe spins in the opposite direction.

On warm days people tend to be much more adventurous and it can lead to a swim.

Games

These games are a fun way to get to know what you and the canoe are capable of.

Sharing paddles is a great game and one of my favourite introductions to the canoe. The rules are simple: each boat has two paddles and four hands. Each paddle must have at least two hands on it and at least one from each person. Don't limit yourself; be imaginative. It's a great way to introduce teamwork.

In the ***confidence lean*** game, toes or feet must be well hooked under the gunwale, seat or thwart. Bum and hands on the opposite gunwale. Talk, coordinate and lean back. The aim is to get your heads in the water.

In ***gunwale bobbing***, knees are bent then straightened to make the canoe squirt forward. If standing on the gunwale seems a little bold, stand just in front of the rear seat and bounce. It still works. Working with children, I some times pair them up with them both standing at the rear of the boat on the floor of the canoe.

I would normally get youngsters to wear helmets. With teenagers and older folk, I use my discretion. Falls from the gunwales tend to be dynamic with the canoe shooting off in the opposite direction. The risk is hitting another canoe rather than your own. Having a lot of space between canoes provides safety.

With the **_leap frog_** game you start by sitting as far back as you can so that the bow goes high. Run at the other canoe and, with the help of its paddlers, go over the top. Look after your fingers and don't get them trapped between the canoes. If you are supervising a group, don't let them get too crazy. Some will hurtle up the canoe, carelessly smacking the others with the paddle.

All aboard! How many can you get in the boat and still go paddling? Awareness is important. As the group got into the canoe, two stuck outstretched legs below thwarts and seats. I stopped them and made sure legs were clear. I wanted them to be able to come out of the canoe easily when the inevitable happened.

Ah, warm days. It seems the objective is more about getting wet than going canoeing.

Count heads. If the canoe has capsized then immediately spin it upright to check. All of us have miscounted groups, so make sure the canoe is empty.

The sun burning through.

Flat Water & Lakes

" *I lay snug in my sleeping bag; it was barely light. Other than Lina's gentle breathing, only the long rising call of the loon broke the stillness of morning.*

Quietly I stuck an arm out from my warm cocoon and unzipped the tent. The ground was covered with the fine dew and the countless sparkling spiders' webs gave everything a fairy charm. The river was perfectly still, with a perfect reflection of trees and sun; even the previous night's beaver was not to be seen.

The sun was just visible through the mist. It was going to burn through. I shook Lina awake. This was an opportunity par excellence; we would dance in the sun's reflection. The loon wailed again sending a shiver down my spine – or was that the chill of morning? I woke Steve and Mike; this was an experience not to be missed.

The photographer acted as air traffic controller to guide each canoe into the reflected sun. The beauty and stillness brought out the best paddling in us. Even water dripping from the blade seemed noisy. I kept my blade deep and silent as I swung the canoe from c-stroke to Indian to hanging draw. I lost myself into the dance.

The crack of tinder being broken sounded across the water followed by the first waft of wood smoke. Coffee and pancakes would be soon on the way. I slid the canoe into the reed-fringed shore; it was going to be a good day. "

Do I paddle alone? As an experienced paddler, of course I do. I am fully aware of the risks and plan accordingly.

The Dangers of Open Water

A lake can appear to be the most idyllic of paddling locations. Much of the time it is, but after a sudden change in the weather its character can change in minutes. Keep your eyes open and your senses attuned, and be prepared to change your plans if the weather changes.

There is safety in numbers in that you can help each other out. If you are on your own and something goes wrong are you going to be able to sort it? If you are a short distance from the side, the answer is probably 'yes'. If you are in the middle of a large lake then you could be in very serious trouble. Two canoes are a sensible minimum.

The following photos were taken in a safe location. There was a breeze but even the most inexperienced paddler could make progress into it. The only consequence of the paddler losing contact with his canoe was a great deal of amusement. It did serve to remind us all how quickly a boat and swimmer can be separated in wind, however. On open water we have to show a great deal of caution. As the **_wind_** picks up, I will be kneeling. In very strong winds, where upset is possible, I brief group members on what to do. They must be low in the boat. It is vital they retain a grip on the canoe if they capsize. Even an upside down air-bagged boat will move swiftly.

Bob was gunwale bobbing and fell in. He was swimming fast but the breeze pushed the boat along; within seconds the gap was too great.

In the shelter of a bay the wind does not give a true picture, although the tiny ripples close to shore are an indicator of strong winds.

Right, the same force wind with the effect of fetch.

It is so easy to be lulled into a false idea of waves when launching from the sheltered end of a lake or loch. Waves will build with the **fetch** (the length of water the wind runs across). They will not reach their maximum size until many kilometres down the way. Canoes are vulnerable on open water, as it is easy to take on water in a big or steep sea.

Surf is a dangerous place to be in a canoe. Even a canoe empty of gear will be a danger if swamped. Don't be in the way of it rolling into a beach; it will contain upwards of half a tonne of water. Get out of the boat's way by any means possible. Show caution in landing in large waves.

Lake water can be very cold even as the weather warms up. It may be sunny and the air warm, but water will rob heat from you 25 times faster than air on **immersion**. Your ability to swim will be greatly reduced. Strong swimmers unused to cold waters can react with real shock and panic to immersion.

Extremely **cold water** quickly makes the hands ineffective. I did some training in the midst of winter, when the water temperature was just above freezing. We were trying out rescues for rafted canoes and, although we were in drysuits, our hands were exposed. One rescue failed and we immediately tried a second. It failed and we hastily swam to the beach. My hands had become unusable. As the blood and feeling came back I was reduced to tears from the pain.

The World Heritage Pontcysyllte Aqueduct; ok, its not open water, but the drop is around 40m. Falling to your death from a canoe would be a unique end.

If a person is suddenly dropped into very cold water without a drysuit, the temperature can cause an involuntary response known as **cold shock** bringing on uncontrolled rapid breathing, immediate constriction of surface blood vessels, an increase in heart rate and a surge in blood pressure. These are unpleasant effects for any of us but can, for some, lead to a heart attack or stroke. These effects decline after about 3 minutes, but by then the body will be cooling which will, if the situation is not resolved, lead to hypothermia.

Prolonged immersion will lead to hypothermia and eventual unconsciousness. If a person is unconscious, a BA will not guarantee that they float face up. Once unconscious, a person will drown unless a companion keeps their mouth clear of the water.

When the water is cold, build up experience gradually and be far more cautious about your abilities. Get on your knees and make the boat more stable. Keep close to the shore. Ask the questions: might it go wrong? What will I do if it does? What are the consequences?

If swimming to the side or self rescue are not an option and you are stuck in the water, try to lessen the heat loss. If alone, adopt the **Heat Escape Lessening Position** (HELP). Ankles are crossed. Legs drawn up to protect the groin. Arms are kept tucked to cover the armpits. On no account kick or attempt to generate heat. This will circulate water and cause you to lose heat faster. In a group you should huddle and twine together for the same purpose. Those who carry a polythene exposure bag advocate climbing into that in the water. Things are pretty desperate if you are contemplating these measures.

Anyone who has been in the water for a long period of time and is suffering from **hypothermia** must be treated with extreme care. Water pressure on the legs will have squeezed blood out of circulation. People should not be raised vertically out of the water, as this will encourage blood quickly back into the legs; this can prove fatal. Medical assistance is required fast and the casualty kept horizontal.

The passage of a thunderstorm or weather front will often bring strong and gusty winds or squalls.

Paddling in the middle of a lake during a thunderstorm and being the highest thing for hundreds of metres is not good, as it may prove attractive for the lightening. Whenever possible I will be on the shore. In a mountainous area or hilly country, most strikes will be on high ground or crests. The normal advice is not to shelter beneath trees, but that may be a problem in a forest. In a flatter landscape that is wooded, clear areas and campsites may be situated on rocky knolls so there is not a lot you can do. But I certainly won't be sheltering below a tree on a knoll.

Look out for signs of ***changes in weather***. In the photo to the right a hat was used to obscure the sun. A thin veil of cloud was beginning to cover the sky. This halo confirms that it was cirro-stratus which is often the harbinger of a weather front. During the day, other cloud bands thickened and lowered. The warm front arrived the next morning, bringing the start of a period of poor weather. It is worth using a book, listening to forecasts and gradually building your own forecasting skills. This will stand you in good stead for when you do that remote wilderness trip.

Wildlife can present its own excitement. It can be calm and beguiling up to the point where it decides to protect itself, offspring or territory. Problems with animals will vary from country to country. Be sensible and heed local advice.

What to Carry

Sorting gear for the Bonnet Plume River in NW Canada, a 360 mile wilderness journey.

You may be loading up for a multi-day trip or just be out for a gentle paddle, so what you need to carry will vary massively. Any spare clothing and equipment can be carried in dry bags or barrels. Unless I am paddling in a very confined area, I will normally carry some kit with me. You need to consider the following points.

- How far are you from a road or path?

- What weather are you expecting?

- What time is it going to get dark?

- Do you need spare clothing in the event of a ducking?

- Do you need to look after others?

For longer journeys I will carry a **repair kit**. Seats or their bolts may break; a hull can be split or punctured. The kit shown here contains: gaffer tape[1] for binding or patching; spare seat bolt[2] along with a multi-tool[3] and adjustable spanner[4]; two-part glue[5] for fixing paddles (particularly handles on plastic paddles); cord[6];cable ties for binding[7]; lighter[8]; vinyl repair kit[9]; and needle and cotton[10].

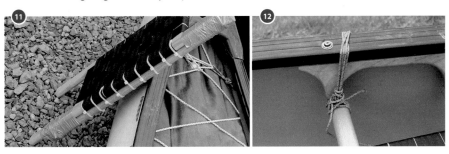

[11] A broken seat has been splinted with an extra piece of wood and bound with cable ties and gaffer tape.

[12] A broken seat bolt has been repaired with cord fastened to the lacing on the outside. We could have removed the broken bolt and threaded the hole with cord.

In easy places or conditions, our dry bags or rucksacks can be **carried loose** in the bottom of the canoe.

You can attach your **kit on a leash** to the canoe. With the gear loose but leashed, you can move it to assist or change the trim. This is useful in windy conditions where the bow needs to be lower into the water. The cord is fastened to the boat with a releasable knot. This works well with just a single bag, but if there are several then you end up with a lot of rope. You can tie one bag to the other in a long chain, but this creates entanglement potential.

We can more easily empty a capsized canoe before recovering gear.

Hired canoes often come as bare boats so here the lashing is along the length of the canoe using seats and thwarts.

In strong winds on open water, I like my gear **lashed down**. Should anything ever go wrong, I want the maximum floatation. In the photo above the lash-down uses the cord drilled and threaded down the side of the canoe. The lashing cord is run from side to side and through any available handles or straps on the kit.

The photo on the left was taken on a river, it but it would be the same on open water. The combination of small airbags and lashed-down kit keeps the canoe afloat even when fully swamped. It is difficult to paddle but still manageable. It is unstable, however, so the bow paddler should not cross deck. By keeping a paddle on each side and each paddler leaning to their paddle side, it is possible to keep going.

With so much rope around, there is a risk of entanglement so an easily accessible **knife** is essential.

The canoe was just part of a great day out for Macy. She had her toys and was equally happy playing in the water.

Small paddles allow them to participate, although their efforts can often be more of a hindrance. Be prepared to paddle back for paddles and toys.

Paddling with Children

Introducing children to canoeing is rewarding for all concerned. However, we must be aware of their individual needs. Children are not just little adults. The fit of the lifejacket is very important with a strap to stop it riding up in the water. There is more flotation on the front and behind the head to ensure a small child floats face up.

So how young can you go? In the illustration on the right, Pete's child is less than a year old. Paddling allows Pete to get out and enriches his daughter's experience of the world. Some words of caution: Pete is highly experienced and even then he is being careful. To make sure the canoe is stable he is kneeling and, importantly, he is wearing his own buoyancy aid. The seat is fastened into the canoe but the baby is NOT fastened into the seat. The big strap is for the lifejacket, not the chair. It would be terrifying to see a baby fastened into a canoe. Inexperienced canoeists can be blissfully unaware of the fact that they could capsize. Be realistic about your abilities. If you lack experience, avoid paddling with very young children.

1 Involve children in the paddling and give them every opportunity to be adventurous.

2 I decided to explore the caves but we did not have helmets. I challenged the group to do everything slowly and quietly and not hit the walls with boat, paddle or self. Nobody banged their head, and they had fun learning to manoeuvre.

3 Some will have greater needs. My nephew Nikhil has learning difficulties and little strength in his hands. I am kneeling to keep the boat stable; I could also rock the canoe to his delight.
Nikhil finds it hard to grip the paddle and has to have his hand underneath to support it. We have got him a lighter paddle and it is possible to adapt it to enable a better grip.

Give some thought to where you are paddling. Landowners can be unhappy about dogs not being on a lead once ashore.

In warmer weather and easier conditions we do not use a BA as Dillie is a good swimmer.

Dogs

Some dogs take to water and others loathe it. Whether your pooch will take to paddling is ultimately up to the dog rather than up to you. Introduce it gently, and don't force the pace.

Dog buoyancy aids are readily available. A handle on the top is necessary to lift a dog back into the canoe, but the one top right has a big loose loop. If the dog swam near branches there would be a chance of being snagged. Under no circumstances tie a dog into a boat. Tied to a capsized canoe, a dog may drown. The one middle right has a neater handle. The little ring is a glowstick from a night paddle.

Dogs love being on the airbags. A tough cover or piece of closed cell foam on the bag can protect it. I buy tough bags and over the years my dog Dillie has only holed one. Dogs get cold. Snow, rain and low temperatures may make your dog's life misery. Dillie has her own sleeping mat and blanket.

Dealing with a Capsize

Capsizing on flat water is no big deal. The important thing is to be able to empty and get back into your canoe. At the bank, a capsized canoe is best emptied in water that is at least knee-deep. By tipping it on its side and then lifting slowly, only the weight of the canoe is lifted and not water.

If the swimmer is agile you can get them into your canoe. However, there is a risk that they may capsize you. Where things are serious, you are a long way from shore and the water is cold, the swimmer stays in the water until the canoe is emptied. Do not risk a further capsize.

In any **deep water rescue**, such as the **curl** shown here, the rescuer takes control. The swimmer holds onto their canoe so as not to be separated. The swimmer is placed on the opposite side of the rescuer's canoe to the capsized canoe, which is gently tipped onto its edge. Using the capsized canoe as a balancing aid, the rescuer stands. The legs are spaced across the canoe but hips and shoulders are square to the white canoe. The back and arms are straight. The legs are doing the lifting. Lifting steadily, the water flows out of the canoe rather than being lifted.

The final lift is a jerk and arms bend. The top gunwale of the emptied canoe is thrown away from the rescuer. He immediately drops down into his own canoe and grabs the empty canoe. The swimmer works around to the far side while keeping hold of the boats. This is a habit to build for windy conditions. The gunwale is lowered to the water enabling the swimmer to pull himself across his own canoe. The rescuer pushes down on the gunwale of the canoe, levelling it and scooping the swimmer into it.

A variation of this is a curl into an *X rescue.* This and a number of other variations are illustrated below.

Keiron lifts the canoe by the painter. He has got the swamped canoe up onto his and begins to tip it over. With the canoe in the X position it is flipped upright.

Helen and Alan pull the canoe across in the X position before flipping it upright.

If someone is struggling to get back in you can use a flooded canoe, which is lower, to scoop them up. You then transfer them to your canoe before emptying the other.

Some will prefer not to stand to do rescues and many are taught the **kneeling X** rescue as their first rescue method. The difficult part is the initial lift when you are trying to break suction as well as the weight of the canoe. Once the canoe is across the rescuer's canoe then it is flipped upright and slid back into the water ready for recovering a swimmer. It is difficult to protect the back as you lean and twist to the side, which is why I prefer to do a standing curl rescue.

If everyone falls in you are faced with an **all-in rescue**. In the above photo sequence, it is being done in easy conditions. One of the paddlers is already swimming in with his painter. The red canoe is turned upright and the gunwale on the far side lowered to get the bow of the green up and onto it. The green canoe is pulled across the red, making an X and a stable platform. The nearest paddler can use the painter and put his feet against the side. Two of the paddlers hold onto the canoes while the third paddler climbs into the red which has enough buoyancy to support him. The top (green) canoe is then flipped upright. With one dry boat the other canoes can be emptied using a normal X or curl rescue.

It may happen in easy conditions but it is more likely to be awful. In the following illustration the wind is gusting to force 5 or 6. The fetch is only a couple of hundred metres at this point but already the waves are building and white horses are forming. Although heavily laden the canoe supports the same rescue. The person in the water must hold onto the canoes.

The method advocated with no air bags is to keep both canoes upside down and use the air trapped in the bottom canoe to support the second. At this point you are meant to throw one edge up and over to turn the top canoe upright. It works with empty boats in reasonable conditions. In difficult conditions, with a strong wind and with laden boats you may not be able to throw the canoe over. To get around the problem you can use a strop.

Ray has fastened a 3m strop (kept in a BA pocket) to the far side of the upturned canoe. He pushes up from the far side, Bob has his feet against the top canoe and leans back pulling on the strop which rotates the canoe upright.

If you end up in the water on your own you will need to hang on to your canoe, empty it and get back in by performing a **solo deep-water** re-entry. Keep your legs on the surface as you try to pull across the canoe. Let them sink and it does not work. At the critical moment, kick water like a Mississippi paddle steamer.

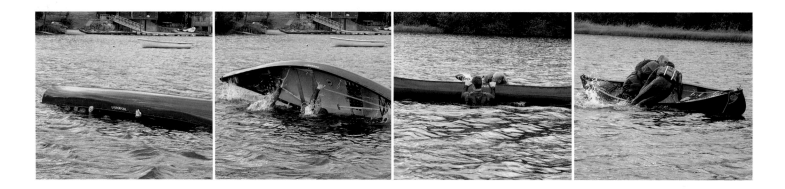

Using the **Capistrano flip** it is possible (but not easy) to throw an empty capsized canoe back upright with a minimum of water being left in the boat. The paddlers go back under the boat and, with a mighty kick of the legs and a thrust with one arm, the canoe is thrown upright. Having got the canoe empty and upright, they then help each other to get back into the canoe one at a time.

Flooded rafted boats will still support the crew as long as they have sufficient buoyancy from air bags or lashed-in kit. If the swamping was caused by large waves on an open lake, water will continue to wash in. The raft may be paddleable, although slow and difficult to manoeuvre. It may be possible to paddle to shore or quieter water where a **_raft rescue_** can be attempted.

A sling or rope is attached to one edge of the raft and the paddlers stand on the opposite gunwale. By a combination of sinking the gunwale of the canoe they are standing on and pulling on the strop, the far canoe begins to tilt upwards. Be careful not to pull the raft right over. Most of the water will flow out of the upper canoe, which the paddlers step into. There is little freeboard in the flooded canoe, so bailing should be fast. Any spare bodies could be used to pull down on the gunwale behind the paddlers to give more freeboard in the full boat. This is a very limited technique and depends on you getting to calmer waters.

If the canoes have no buoyancy in them then a double flip may work. Do this as for the first part of the above method, but pull the canoes right over on top of you so the raft is upside down. Then flip again and, hopefully, one canoe will be empty.

Towing

The ability to assist a companion by towing them is critical. It enables us to deal with a situation before it becomes serious and is one of the skills which enables groups of paddlers to be independent and to look out for each other.

A simple and effective **V assist**: the canoes are not tied together. The bows touch and both paddlers apply power on the outside of the V. Steering is achieved by applying more power on one side or the other or the occasional steering stroke. The boats can get out of line, so just reach across and pull them back into the V.

In any towing situation some form of **quick-release** method must be used to attach the towing boat to the tow rope. A quick and simple method involves taking a couple of wraps around a thwart and placing a knee or foot on the end of the rope.

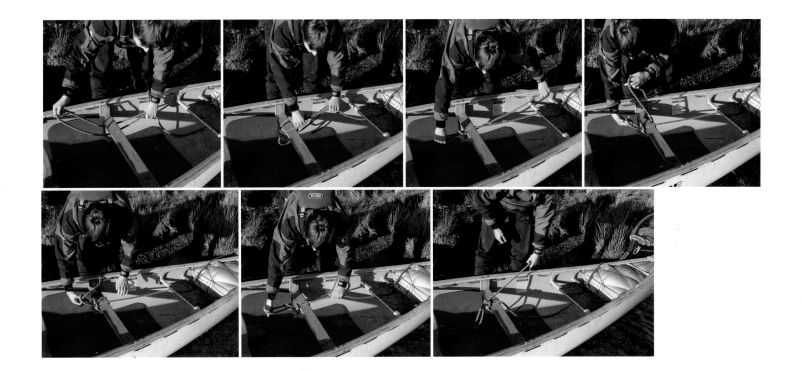

Over a distance on flat water, most paddlers use a releasable knot for attaching a tow. Any method of release must be quick and reliable under load.

A highwayman's hitch is a good quick-release hitch. The 'load' rope is the section of rope heading directly to the towed boat. A bight of rope (posh name for a loop) is passed under a thwart. A hand is passed into the loop and grips the load rope. A loop of the load rope is pulled back through the bight.

Push some fingers through the new loop and grip the non-load rope. Pull it through to make a new loop. Pull tight on the load rope. To release, pull on the non-load rope. In the above sequence the towrope is passed under the seat of the

In awkward or dangerous situations, you may need to ditch the towed boat fast.

Solo paddlers pair up to head upwind. The painter from the towed boat is fastened in the other.

In a whitewater rescue I only use the wrap and knee method. Releasing a knot could be too slow.

stern paddler and attached ahead of him on the thwart. Done like this, the rope does not obstruct the paddle. A sailing jam cleat is another effective and releasable method that some use. All methods of towing must be releasable under load. Do not use non-releasable knots.

Linking boats is a useful method because it allows an experienced paddler in the rear boat to steer and move a less able group windwards. The painter is taken around the mid-thwart, threaded back along the canoe and through the carrying handle. It then goes around the mid-thwart of the second canoe with a double wrap. The second paddler kneels on the tape to fasten it off. The bow of the second canoe must be pulled tight to the first. The canoes can now be paddled as a single unit.

Several canoes have been linked by the same method. It requires a good front and stern paddler and all systems are releasable.

Coping with the Wind

In the wind we need a clear understanding of how we use both the trim and our paddle strokes to maintain control. On large expanses of water we can end up in seriously dangerous situations. Understanding how our canoe works can ease our progress and, as long as we do not overestimate our ability, we can have a lot of fun.

The five photos below illustrate how the wind affects the canoe (a light wind is blowing onshore): the boat is slightly bow light[1]; Ray has moved to the stern of the canoe and so the bow is high[2]; the canoe acts as a weather vane and swings downwind[3]; the canoe has finished its swing and Ray is moving to the bow[4]; with the bow heavy, the boat again swings to point downwind with the light end[5].

Ten-year-old Chris has moved back to make the canoe stern heavy; as a result he can run downwind with control and ease.

When running with strong **_tail winds_** we steer with stern rudders. J strokes are not as effective and tend to lock the body over the paddle, unbalancing us.

In a **_side wind_**, by paddling on the downwind side[1] you can use the push of the wind on the light bow to counter the turning element of the power stroke. By moving backwards or forwards you find a balance point for these two forces. You can keep a straight line simply by changing the trim, which is my preferred method in a side wind. When paddling tandem you have to experiment but, in strong tail winds, the bow paddler can move into the middle of the canoe to ease the steering. The same effect can be achieved by paddling on the upwind side with the stern light[2].

To turn from a tail-heavy run, change the trim. In the sequence[3], the paddler slides to the middle of the boat and uses an outside pivot turn to head upwind.

In **headwinds** you can travel in the windward direction with the boat either slightly bow light or just level trimmed[4]. As things get even windier, I prefer to be just bow heavy; I will stop steering and swap sides every four or five strokes. When going into a strong wind while paddling in tandem, it is good to switch sides frequently.

At times the wind will get too strong for us to make any sensible progress. On an expedition we may have to camp and wait. If the shore is reasonably unobstructed, we have the option of **tracking into the wind**. In the sequence below the boat is set up with a large loop of rope fastened from the bow to the stern. All the weight is in the downwind end of the canoe. The canoeist sets out at a run with the canoe pre-angled which takes the canoe out. Once the canoe is out, the combination of the wind and the bite into the water means it can be flown like a kite. He can now slow down and move to windward. The angle can be lessened to make the drag less, which helps the canoe bite into the water if it has some weight in it.

In strong winds you can track if being blown offshore is a dangerous proposition. Avoidance is better than cure, and tracking can be a safe alternative to paddling.

You can also alter the trim by moving your pack further forwards.

A group is taking a break from paddling into a headwind.

The wind was Force 5 and it was hard work holding onto the handle. In that wind we were not keen to tie the brolly to the canoe.

Improvised Sailing

In a 19th-century sketch, George Catlin shows Native Americans enjoying a canoe race; he commented that the men stood in the bows of the canoes stretching blankets out as sails while the women steered. Small boat and wind are an intoxicating temptation for fun; you are only limited by your imagination.

The location is safe with warm water and the bank easily in reach.

The sail has pockets on the top corners to hold paddles or poles. The bottom is split with each point having a buckle fastened to the seat.

When **_rafted sailing_** we can build bigger sailing rigs. It is exciting and practical, but be aware of the dangers. As the fetch increases, so do the waves.

Here, a log is used as a crosspiece. The cord is tied off to the thwart with a clove hitch and is wrapped tightly around both thwart and log. The cord is wrapped horizontally around all of the vertical binding. This tightens everything up, and then the end of the rope is tied off with another clove hitch. The raft is completed by tying the ends of the canoes. It helps to pull the bows in tighter than the stern; many believe that this dissipates the wave that is created between the boats.

Poles are used for the A-frame. Taking the cord back across the middle tightens the binding on the slippery aluminium. With wood, the wraps around should be sufficient. The green binding is completed and finished off by tying it to the pole with a clove hitch. An overhand on the bight is tied in the loose end of the green rope and a karabiner attached. The blue rope is put into the karabiner and will become the halyard for hauling up the sail. The yellow rope is clove hitched to the pole and will be used to hold the frame up.

One kilometre down Llyn Tegid and the waves are beginning to build.

Sometimes I use two logs, one at the back of each seat. Some people reckon that the single crosspiece is better as the canoes move independently. I use both systems, but choose the two-crosspiece method in windier conditions as it seems more secure.

In some settings I will collect wood from the forest (I do not cut wood poles in the UK; it takes little to destroy the remaining wild places).

The frame is in place and the yellow rope holds it up. An overhand on the bight is put into the yellow rope and the rope is then run through the ends of the canoe and back up and through the loop. Everything is tightened and the yellow rope fastened off with half hitches. The bottoms of the poles are fastened off to the seats with wraps and cross bindings. The poles can cause wear marks on the plastic, so you may want to improvise some padding.

A tarp is being used as a sail. The top edge has been gathered in to make a triangular sail and is now fastened to the blue rope. There is rope from each of the other two corners that will be used to control the sail. The group have put the sail behind the yellow rope (although I would normally have it in front). The canoe is being steered from the back with a stern rudder and it can be useful to use a bow jam to push the front across the wind.

The rig can be built with more canoes.

It can get wild out there and inevitably you will be starting where the waves are smaller. Surfing metre-high waves is not a good place to learn the lessons; being rafted may even increase the risk.

A friend placed the A-frame too far forward and then used a parachute as a sail. The canoe pitch poled; the bows buried and stopped dead, The canoes reared up to a steep angle before swamping.

The photo above shows a very simple rafted rig. There is no crosspiece and the canoes are just tied together. This works well as a raft, but would be more prone to taking in waves and splashes in very windy conditions. One paddler holds the upright pole wrapping his leg around the pole to act as a mast foot. A paddler in the stern holds the yellow rope and the two hold ropes from the bottom corners of the sail. It is quick and effective, and even easier with more people. The top fastening is done with a throw bag. The rope is clove-hitched around the pole just below the bag and fastened to the sail.

▎▎ *With three people in each canoe, we took part in a charity canoe race and run. We had the biggest spinnaker sail we could get hold of. We were in the lead as we screamed up the Mawddach estuary. I had briefed the two holding the sail to let go if it was necessary to de-power. The bow wave was peaking about two-thirds of the way along the hull just centimetres below the gunwale. Our speed increased and the wave flooded in. I shouted to let the sail go but both holders were sailors and started bundling the*

Person overboard: make sure everyone is aware of this deadly danger and that they show real caution in moving about. If it does happen, ditch the sail immediately; do not turn the raft. Get everyone to spin on the spot, face the other way and paddle back. In a strong wind this may not work, so avoidance is crucial.

spinnaker rather than releasing. It kept the power on for critical seconds. We swamped and were swimming.

We were fortunate enough to be swept onto a sandbank, and we resumed with caution. On expedition, I have all the kit lashed down so in the event of a swamping we would still be afloat and able to paddle.

This rig uses a split pole. The mast fits into one sleeve and the gaff into the diagonal.

Sailing Rigs

With a few simple modifications you can increase the versatility of the canoe.

The rig is mounted to the rear of the bow seat. We need a mast foot and something to hold the mast at seat or gunwale level. A separate thwart can be used to hold the mast. Mounting it at gunwale level makes the set-up strong but it does mean that you can no longer use the bow seat back to front as a solo paddler. A mast foot can be a carved wooden block and heavy-duty fabric formed into a tube or some kind of adapted rubber fitting. Glues need to be chosen carefully, as the wrong epoxy can destroy Royalex.

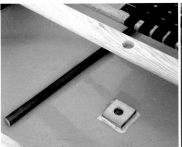
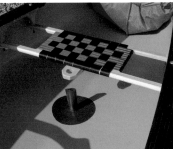

A Munson Ring, designed to hold pipes to a wall, makes a great mast mounting. Unscrewing the ring leaves the seat usable.

A simple clamp can be added over a seat and tightened or removed with the wing nut.

Running across the wind the sail is hauled in. The paddle is placed on the down-wind side to act as a leeboard; this stops the hull skidding downwind. By moving the paddle backwards or forwards you can control the direction. Too far forwards and it begins to turn the canoe to windward; if you are not careful, it will stall.

For stability crosswind, I lie along the floor of the canoe with my head towards the mast. The sheet (the rope from the corner of the sail) is taken back through the seat and then forwards to a turn around a thwart ahead of me. In light wind I may use a releasable knot to hold the sheet but, as the wind increases, I hold the rope in my hand for an instant easing or release. Some add sailing jam cleats to do this job.

These two leeboards are shown together for comparison; only one is used in practice. Photo courtesy of Solwaydory.co.uk

As the rigs become bigger they become more efficient and it even becomes possible to tack to windward with the addition of a leeboard. A leeboard is a sheet of wood that is hung over the side and provides lateral resistance (without which a boat cannot travel to windward), effectively giving the canoe a keel.

On the right is a clip-on leeboard that can be moved to the downwind side of the canoe. The leeboard on the left is mounted on a swivel and is only used on the one side of the canoe. Because of this, it is longer than the transferable leeboard.

It was finally time for the big crossing over the Irish Sea to Wales. We set out paddling from Dun Laoghaire at 7.08 am and Dave and I weaved our way out through the moored sailing boats. Once out of shelter, we hoisted the sail and were underway towards the lighthouse on the northern end of the Kish Bank.

We were 6 miles out to sea and the flood tide was running strongly across the banks. The first breakers climbed above the stern, spilling water down onto us. I worked to keep us

Thirty miles from land: Dave Howie midway on our Irish Sea Crossing. A leeboard is hanging to the left.

stern-to-the-worst while controlling the sail at the same time, while Dave bailed hard and fast. We passed the lighthouse and were clear of the banks, out into the open sea. The pursuing westerly wind was driving us towards the Welsh coast.

Ireland disappeared behind us. The wind dropped and backed into the south just as forecast; with the leeboard over the side we were making slow but steady progress.

Eventually there was a line of clouds ahead; they had to be the mountains of Snowdonia. After hours of straining eyes, the distinct shape of Holyhead Mountain was recognisable. We were, at last, able to confirm my navigational plan.

At the speed we were doing, we would reach Anglesey during the flood tide and in the early hours of the morning. Going through the tide races during the flood in this wind was not even an option. We would have to delay landing until the tide eased.

The South Stack lighthouse became visible in the distance, followed by the double flash of the Skerries. Eventually the wind dropped and the sea quietened.

There was a moment of apprehension as a large ship bore down on us, its lights clearly visible. Dave shone his torch onto the sail and I held mine steadily at the approaching lights. Suddenly we were bathed in the glare of a searchlight. They appeared to be waiting for a signal from us; I kept the torch steady. The ship continued past and we were alone again.

Bearings on South Stack light showed that we were travelling backwards and, even though I had planned it that way, it was demoralising. We could do nothing but wait until 2 am and the ebb tide, when we could turn and head towards Anglesey once more.

The wind strengthened yet again so I let the sail swing ahead of the mast, spilling out wind. We were heading into Trearddur Bay. We cranked the sail back in, the speed of the boat matching our need to be back on land. Water broke in front of us and we shot through a gap in a reef. I frantically rushed the sail down and grabbed a paddle. We passed by more rocks, and then came a break in the cliff to our right. A dozen more *strokes and were in calm water, weaving once more through gently bobbing sailing boats and dinghies.*

At 4.20 am that morning there were no coherent thoughts to be had, just an embrace. We were both swaying on the dry land, which was strangely still. We had just sailed an open canoe from Ireland to Wales. We pulled everything above the tide line and fell into an exhausted sleep.

A variety of rigs are illustrated above. The photo on the right shows a rig used for downwind running. This rig is clipped to the canoe and then held upright by a couple of cords. The rigidity is given by a 'perimeter batten', which can be twisted or bent but returns to its circular shape. The sail is coiled into thirds for stowage.

Night Paddling

You may decide to paddle during a beautiful night or may have been caught out by nightfall. In either case, it is important to have a light source and be visible to your companions. Be prepared for the eventuality and keep head torches and light sticks accessible.

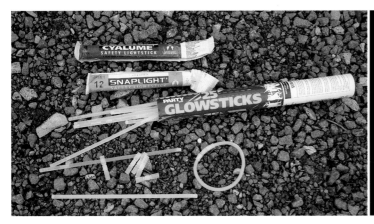

As night draws in the reflective patches on the BA and jacket come into their own.

Many BAs come with reflective strips which make them far more visible. A head torch will enable you to see ahead on the darkest of nights and keep your hands free. There may be enough light to negate the use of the torch, but it can be on the head in readiness. A small light stick can be looped around the shoulder strap.

Light sticks are a good way of making everyone easier to spot. The top two are powerful and visible at a great distance. However, they do tend to ruin night vision and are relatively expensive. The 'party' glow sticks are cheap and come with a connector to turn them into a circle. The glow is enough to see people, but not really bright enough to affect vision. They can be attached to the front and back of the BA. The higher the attachment, the easier it will be to spot a swimmer.

A numbering system is useful with a larger group. The leader will be 1 and the rest will number off from there. Once the system is in place, when the leader shouts "1!" the rest can follow in sequence, hence checking that all are there. Boats can buddy up. Front or back markers can be helpful.

If you are leading a group, position yourself to make visual checks easy. This is often to the side rather than the front of the group. I only go to the front when I am concerned about what is ahead.

Strokes

By defining, separating and naming strokes, we risk separating them in our head and in our practice. We end up with a draw stroke followed by a power stroke followed by a steering stroke, instead of a continuous whole. We need to separate them to make them manageable in terms of learning and refining them; we should always remember that, when manoeuvring, a blend of strokes is required. Where alternative stroke names are in common usage I have made a note of this.

Strokes and manoeuvres can be done on-side, off-side or cross-deck. The on-side is where one would naturally paddle; off-side is the other side. Cross-deck refers to bringing the paddle across the canoe to use on the off-side without swapping hand positions. An inside turn is to the on-side. An outside turn is towards the off-side. The drive or power face of the blade is the one pulling back against the water when doing a forward power stroke; the back face is the other.

The bow and stern paddlers must clearly understand their respective roles. Paddling harmoniously requires work, and canoes are not known as 'divorce boats' for nothing. For big corrections and turns, the bow paddler is needed. Often it is the bow that initiates these moves, but both ends should work in harmony. Both must understand what is going on. There is nothing worse than a bow paddler who only puts strokes in at the command of the stern paddler. They are learning little other than how to follow orders.

When running straight, all of the steering should be done in the stern. For most tandem crews, the canoe will turn towards the bow paddler's paddling side, necessitating a correction stroke at the stern at the end of most power strokes.

When going into a headwind tandem, a bow paddler may need to do an occasional quick correction to assist. Too much correction at the bow leads to a lack of power (and irritation to the stern paddler).

Keeping in a Straight Line

Getting the boat started and running straight can be difficult for the novice. Using vertical power strokes helps but, unless our canoe has a substantial keel, we need to be able to keep the boat straight by using a steering stroke to bring it back on course.

The **stern rudder** is the simplest steering stroke. It comes into its own running down a lake with a strong tail wind. It is used in whitewater along with its derivative, the stern pry.

The canoe must be moving forwards. By pushing the blade away from the canoe the turn is towards the paddle side. By pulling the blade back in towards the canoe and pushing the leading hand outwards, the canoe starts to turn away from the blade side. Knees are pointing towards the working side and, during the stroke, the torso rotates further to that side. Once you have learnt the stroke, your attention should be on where you are going and not the blade.

With the stern rudder, there is however a time lapse between the effective application of forwards power, which takes place forwards of the knees, and the steering behind your body. This means it is difficult to keep pace with a bow paddler and steering will be relatively slow. The J stroke will answer this problem.

Get someone else to give the canoe a good push to get it running straight. You can then practise the stroke.

The **stern sweep** gives a powerful turn away from the paddler's side while still keeping up forward momentum. We can use this stroke to initiate or continue a turn, or if we wish to run straight, we can use it as a correction stroke. If we just do the last part of the stroke to the stern (the most powerful part), then it is often termed a **stern draw**.

The photo sequence begins with the stern paddler's paddle extended out at right angles to the stern paddler. The paddle blade then begins to form a quarter-circle just below the surface. A lot of the power is being generated by the torso rotation to the paddling side. In the final photo, the torso is fully rotated and the final kick is given by punching the forward hand across the chest and out to the left side (on-side) of the canoe. This is very important as the real power is in the final move of the blade to the stern. Just before the blade hits the boat, it is sliced up and out of the water.

Stern sweep in a tandem canoe.

Forward Paddling

The essence of forward paddling is that the paddle is steep during the power phase. In the above photo the paddlers are in sync for efficiency, and we can clearly see the steepness of the paddle as it is brought back through the power phase.

When forward paddling, we want to be efficient: the big muscles of the torso should do the work and not the smaller ones in the arms. With the blade horizontal, the paddle is swung forward to its full extent. The right shoulder (shoulder on paddle side) goes from slightly back to some way forward; this is the wind up[1]. The paddle is swung upright. At this point it is driven down to engage the water[2]. The torso unwinds. The right shoulder moves from forward to back. The power is transferred from the body to the paddle, and the arms have done relatively little. Once the hands come past the knees, little effective power is transferred. The paddle then goes further back to steer or else exits the water[3].

I have been soaked on a number of occasions by inexperienced but enthusiastic and inefficient bow paddlers. Wrongly, they apply massive power behind the hip, lifting water and shovelling it, with great gusto, into the canoe. The canoe should travel smoothly through the water. However, if the bow paddler does not have a steep paddle at the start, they will lift the bow. Continuing power transfer behind the hips, they lift water and drive the bow down. The boat will bob its way forwards absorbing energy; this is inefficient.

When viewed head-on, we can clearly see the slice forwards to help the rotation and cut the blade through the air. The paddlers are in-sync and, during the power phase, the paddles are fairly vertical. At the bow, the stroke follows a line parallel to the centreline of the canoe. If the bow paddler were to follow the curve of the gunwale line, it would cause the canoe to turn very slightly to her paddling side. The stern paddler then has to do extra unnecessary steering and may not stay in-sync. With the stroke parallel, the bow runs into clean water. When the stroke follows the gunwale, the canoe runs into disturbed water and slides slightly that way. A good parallel stroke from the bow eases the job of the stern paddler: be nice to stern paddlers.

As the adage goes, 'practice makes permanent'; make sure your practice is good.

In the **_J stroke_** the same blade face is used throughout. We take hold of a piece of water, apply power and then, as we turn the blade outwards, we are still using the same water to steer with. The J stroke or 'long J' can at first feel unnatural, but soon you will understand why paddlers as far a-field as the Amazon Basin, the Islands of the Pacific or forests of Canada used the same steering stroke. Once mastered, it feels natural and fluent. Use it in the stern of a tandem canoe or when paddling solo. It is the foundation of a whole group of strokes: Short J, Indian Stroke, Knifed J and C Stroke. It is used for straight running or turning towards the paddle side.

The position of the thumb on top of the paddle is a useful indicator and check. This thumb can be pointing down or up, inwards or outwards.

The paddler's knees are pointed slightly to the paddling side and he is closer to that side. This will ease the stress on the wrist of the top hand. In a tandem canoe, the boat will need to be flat. The canoe is already travelling forwards for this particular version of the J.

In the sequence below as the power phase finishes and the paddle passes your hips, begin to rotate the indicator thumb downwards. You can help this with the bottom hand so the rotation is done with both hands initially. The power face rotates outwards. Do this in a really calm place and you should be able to feel that you are taking one piece of water through from the power element and turning it outwards.

Here the bottom hand is outside the gunwale and the paddler levers off to steer. Sometimes you do not need to use the gunwale, particularly when the steering is easy. When you have done enough, rotate the blade to exit it from the water. This way the blade wants to come out rather than you having to lift it.

How far over we twist the blade and paddle will depend on what we are trying to achieve. The blade is shown out of the water for clarity[1]. It has a steep angle that will give a bite on the water as you push the blade out from the canoe. It is a good angle to initially aim at, as it will feel positive. Below the blade is pitched right up onto its edge[2]. This gives a very powerful steer when pushed out from the boat. It is good starting from stationary. It is also the starting point for the Indian Stroke. It puts stress on the forward wrist so it should not be the normal angle but it is a good one to practise.

When the canoe is running well, and you need less steering, you may use quite a shallow angle on the blade.

Knifed J, from left to right

The **knifed J** is a smooth and elegant stroke. It gives an extra subtlety to the J stroke. After the power phase of the stroke the blade is swept back to a J but, in this case, at a very shallow angle. The blade then cuts back through the water at a shallow angle with the leading edge down. Effectively, you are lifting water without breaking the surface. The blade exits as soon as you have achieved enough of a course correction. Simply increase the angle of the leading edge of the blade, and it jumps into the air. In this sequence of photos the outside hand lifts the blade. The lift can also be achieved by levering off the gunwale as the blade swings forward.

The **short J** is perhaps the quickest of steering strokes. When the boat is already running straight it puts little strain on the body, allows you to match the cadence of a bow paddler and, when needed, to keep up a very fast stroke rate. In whitewater it pairs well with the stern pry; when speed is needed you can finish the power stroke with the appropriate amount of steering but without wasting time with longer steering strokes. For many paddlers, this becomes the normal cruising stroke. Paddles wear out more quickly but there is less stress on the body.

In the sequence above the normal power stroke is done. Effective power due to trunk rotation is finished when the top hand passes the knee, so the sooner you can steer the quicker you can get on with the next stroke. As the paddle passes the hip it begins to slide along the gunwale (you will get a wear point on the paddle). In the final photo, the blade is turning into the J stroke. The bottom hand is above the gunwale.

With the paddle shaft against the gunwale, the top hand pulls inwards in front of the body. At speed this will be a jerk. In this illustration, the conditions are easy and the paddler is not travelling fast; the angle of the blade is therefore relatively low. If accelerating or travelling quickly, the blade may be at a much steeper angle and the stroke quite splashy. Often only part of the blade is used for steering. The blade is then recovered forwards as a slice as you begin to wind the body up for the next power stroke.

If you want to accelerate the canoe then you should not only use rotation but also lean forwards and backwards to use even more trunk muscles. Try to keep the paddle steep and the blade engaged with the water for longer. The steering is done with a stern pry.

This is only used in short bursts so you can practise using a four-stroke combination: the first two are steered with prys and the second two with short Js. It a good way of cementing the association between these steering strokes. (See stern pry on page 119.)

The **_Indian stroke_** is the most beautiful of strokes. It combines grace and silence when we glide towards wildlife or enjoy the stillness of a mirror calm lake. It can provide control in an eddy or in a gusting wind.

After a power stroke, we do a very steep J stroke. The blade is right up on its edge. The bottom hand in this instance is outside the gunwale to take the blade further back to provide more steering (it can be done from a short J). The blade is now being sliced forwards through the water and the top hand has loosened.

The blade continues its slice forwards. Then, as the blade finishes its slice forwards, the top hand re-grips the paddle and the blade is rotated to provide a new power stroke. Each power stroke will be on an alternate blade face.

Do not make the mistake of thinking that the Indian stroke is just about beauty and silence: give it a go with some real 'oomph'.

To achieve silence the stroke has to be done slowly. Noise is created by water running around the throat of the paddle (the area where the blade and shaft join), so we can raise the blade a little out of the water to avoid this. Try a few strokes with your eyes closed in still conditions while holding the paddle with your fingertips. It is the most sensual of strokes. By slicing the blade out during the recovery and pulling it back in as a C-stroke, the Indian can be used as a powerful and graceful turn.

Turning your Boat

There are a number of strokes that help us to turn the canoe. In this section we will look at the simple and effective strokes.

To perform a solo **_sweep stroke_**, reach forward with the blade and then swing it in a half circle just below the surface. The torso is used to power this swing. Notice how far the paddler's chest has swung around in the last photo. The final part of this stroke leaves the front hand punching out over the side of the canoe. Just before the blade hits the boat it is clipped up and out of the water. Edging towards the stroke speeds up the turn. During a manoeuvre you may need to use only the front (bow sweep) or back (stern sweep) half of the stroke.

An exercise: Repeating the stroke we spin in a circle. Try doing the stroke at different speeds. Use a scale of 1–5 with 1 slow and 5 as fast as you can go. The fastest turn should be when you are operating at 3 or 4. At 5, the blade is not as effective at gripping the water. After a turn or two the paddle blade pretty much stays in the same spot in the water during the stroke, and it is the canoe that moves.

The first part of the **reverse sweep** from the stern is powerful because it uses trunk rotation. However, once we pass the half-way point we start using smaller muscles in the arms for power and the final part to the bow is particularly weak. For the solo paddler, the inside pivot turn is a better progression.

The first part of the **inside pivot turn** (compound reverse sweep) is the same as the reverse sweep with the back of the blade doing the work, the indicator thumb is pointing up. Just before the paddle is at right angles to the canoe the indicator thumb rotates towards the chest and down toward the groin turning the paddle in the process. The arc continues now using the power face of the blade finishing with what is effectively a bow draw. To increase the power the top hand is pushed across the chest to outside the shoulder. The draw is finished at the front of the canoe.

Without swapping hand positions or blade angle the paddle is slashed along the side of the canoe all the way to the stern. This is done at speed to prevent being tripped by the blade. With the blade at the stern you are ready to repeat the sequence.

At the halfway point some will swap the top hand from thumb up to thumb down without rotating the blade in the water. The more you edge towards the stroke the easier the turn.

Sweeps and draws make for a powerful stroke combination for turning the tandem canoe. The bow paddler can use the draw to turn the canoe, turn it on the move or to straighten the canoe up when paddling in strong winds or on whitewater.

Combine a draw stroke at the bow with a stern sweep in the stern. The bow paddler draws into the hip, clipping the blade out just before hitting the canoe. She can use this to turn the canoe on the spot or even if moving at speed. The stern paddler starts level with the hip and sweeps to the stern, putting a real effort into the last part of the stroke. The front hand is slightly elevated which puts the arms into a stronger position.

We can use the **cross-bow draw** solo or when positioned in the bow of a tandem canoe. It gives us a powerful turn at the front of the canoe. The bow paddler raises the paddle horizontally. During this, the indicator thumb will be up. By rotating your chest (it helps if you swivel the knees a bit as well) you swing the paddle to your off-side. The paddle blade is then drawn into the front of the canoe, clipping out of the water just before hitting the boat.

The cross-bow draw can be combined with a reverse sweep in the stern for a powerful turn.

The **outside pivot turn** is performed solo. The combination of a sweep stroke and a cross-bow draw gives a powerful turn on the spot. The canoe is leant slightly towards the paddle for both parts of the stroke. You can start with the sweep or the cross-bow. So as the paddle switches side so does the lean.

Moving Sideways

There are times when we need to move the boat sideways for short distances. These strokes are also important in that they have a number of other uses in more advanced situations.

Kelvin is in a true solo boat, much narrower than most of the canoes shown in the book.

When the canoe has no forward momentum, a ***draw stroke*** with a sliced recovery works well. Your chest is rotated to the stroke. The blade is drawn in as with the simple draw. As the blade gets close to the canoe, the paddle is quickly rotated so the blade can slice back out through the water. This is often referred to as feathering the blade. The indicator thumb, the top hand, is pointing out. Once back out, the blade is turned again for another draw.

Pry with sliced recovery.

A **pry** with a sliced recovery moves you away from the blade. The bottom hand rests on the gunwale and holds the paddle shaft against the side of the canoe. Some paddlers hook their lower thumb over the inside of the gunwale. The blade is then sliced towards the canoe, rotated and levered away. At the end of the pry, and without taking the blade from the water, it is again rotated and sliced back towards the boat. Slice the blade slightly under the canoe for even more power.

The **sculling draw** is an elegant stroke that requires a delicate touch and teaches us to feel the blade. This stroke is so dependent on feel that you should try it with your eyes closed to heighten sensitivity. Try to be really gentle and quiet.

The same blade face is used throughout. Maintaining a steady distance from the canoe, the paddle is moved back and forth. The angle is apparent in the photos. It does not take much of an angle to achieve a sideways movement; too great an angle on the blade is inefficient. The paddle is as upright as is reasonable. Your knees and torso are pointed in the direction of travel. Start the sideways movement with an ordinary draw stroke, then change to the sculling draw. The flatter the canoe, the easier it will move across the water.

If you ever get the chance, step tentatively into a coracle. These have a wooden frame covered in canvas and tar (or traditionally, hide) and it is a little like sitting in the middle of a large soup bowl! The sculling draw pulls it along.

Cross-deck sculling is a very neat way of moving away from your on-side; knees face the off-side. Swing the paddle across the canoe without swapping hands and then scull on the off-side.

Turning on the Move

When the canoe is already moving forwards, we can use strokes that exploit its momentum.

The ***bow rudder*** is a powerful turning stroke done either by the bow or solo paddler. When paddling tandem, the stern paddler should initiate the turn with a sweep stroke. In the sequence we can see that the canoe is turning to the left. The bow paddler has rotated her body to her paddling side and is placing the paddle blade in parallel to the direction of travel. Her blade is fully immersed. She has

turned the leading edge of the blade outwards from the canoe. The water is pulling powerfully at the blade and she has a strong body and arm position to withstand this. The rotation of the chest towards the move is crucial to create strength and protect the shoulders. The canoe is edged towards the turn and there is little the stern paddler can do to help. The boat must be kept edged to the left. This maintenance of the correct edge will be a critical skill on moving water. In the last photo, the bow paddler has sliced her blade further forward and is now drawing it in towards the bow to complete the turning element.

When carried out solo, the bow rudder has to be placed slightly further forwards. This takes the blade past the pivot point of the canoe, i.e. slightly ahead of the paddler. Note the rotation of the body to the paddling side. At the end of the turn the blade is drawn towards the canoe to complete the turn, and then turned into a power stroke.

What's in a name? This stroke goes by a variety of names: *bow rudder*, *bow cut* and *Duffek*. The latter was applied after US slalom paddlers observed the Czech Milo Duffek, who was using turning strokes at the front of his kayak rather than at the back (the norm at that time). This gave him a speed advantage. The American slalomists returned home using and teaching this 'new' stoke, little realising that it had been in use in canoes of the north for millennia.

The **cross-bow rudder** is a bow rudder executed on the off-side. The bow paddler has initiated the turn to the left and the boat is edged to the left. As with a cross-bow draw, the bow paddler has swung her paddle across the canoe. Her indicator thumb is forwards and the power face of the blade is towards the canoe. The blade is put in pretty well parallel to the direction of travel and then gently opened. The leading edge of the blade is then turned away from the canoe. Open it to the pressure you want and which you can hold. Do not put the blade in open: you will jar your shoulder and arms and stall the boat. The blade pulls the bow into the turn. The stern paddler assists with a stern rudder-come-brace. This is a very effective combination on whitewater, which gives a powerful turn with stability.

The bow paddler finishes with a cross-deck power stroke and then switches the paddle back to her on-side. Alternatively, she could have used another cross-bow draw to tighten the turn.

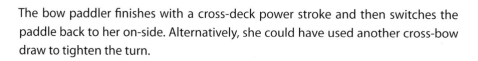

Solo, the turn is initiated with a sweep on the left. The paddler has reached further forwards with the blade, and the shaft slopes forwards. The right arm is tucked and bent, protecting the shoulder from sudden impact. The extreme edge assists the turn. The weight is on your right knee but the left heel is hooked up against the kneeling thwart to give stability. How you finish the move will depend on where you want to go next. In this sequence the blade has been drawn in and is now a cross-deck power stroke. This keeps the power on through the move and starts to straighten the canoe up. At the finish of the stroke, the blade is sliced forwards to exit the water. Another power stroke can be done or the blade swung back to the on-side.

The **_bow jam_** is a bold and dynamic stroke done on the move. It causes a powerful turn away from the bow paddler's on-side. The stern paddler initiates the turn. From a stern rudder, it is easy to tilt the blade over into a low brace to provide stability. The bow paddler slides her blade into the water. The blade is in and pressing hard against the canoe! The canoe turns rapidly away from the blade, but it also tries to capsize to the paddle side. The shaft is against the hull to take the load. At the back of the boat, the stern rudder is tilting over into a brace and the paddler's weight is holding the canoe stable.

" *Dave, Luke and I were running a course for a group of trainee coaches. With Dave in the bow we were looking good as we ran parallel to the beach. Our track was taking us directly towards a very large upturned tree root system at the end of the cove.*

A quiet voice from the front of the canoe came: 'Which way shall we turn?' I gave no answer but kept the power and speed on. Louder, he asked 'Which way?'

If anything, I increased the power from the stern.

'WHICH WA….'

We slammed bow-first into the stump with Dave catapulting forwards onto the airbag. From the shore came a stunned silence. I leant forward towards Dave. 'You're in the front: you decide.' Peels of laughter from the students drowned out any immediate response from Dave (just as well really).

What was the point I was trying to make in my less-than-subtle way? Dave could easily have initiated the turn from the bow with either a bow or cross-bow rudder. I would then have followed and assisted from the stern. At that time, Dave was highly skilled solo boater but had done little in the bow. I considered it a part of his education. Dave has also taught me a fair bit over the years, with a similar amount of subtlety. **"**

Solo bow jam.

There are various ways of doing the bow jam solo and this is my favourite. A gentle sweep initiates the turn. The paddle is then laid horizontally out from the canoe, the blade flat and the indicator thumb pointing outwards. The back face of the blade is skyward. Wait until the flow is directly towards the extended paddle. The blade then goes in and I allow it to rotate and go down under the canoe; the indicator thumb points down at the finish of this. As the blade locks against the canoe, there is a jerk and the turn accelerates (quite unsettling the first time you feel it). As the power diminishes, finish with a bow pry to turn further. Note the paddlers knees spread across the canoe for extra stability.

The **stern pry** is an extremely powerful steering stroke which, with a snappy application, allows us to get on with providing power. It allows the body to lean away from the stroke; vital in some whitewater moves.

The sequence begins with a power stroke. The blade is then brought back to plaster it to the side of the canoe. The tighter the blade is to the hull, the better. The indicator thumb is up. After a brief moment to allow the blade to re-engage the water, you pry the blade outwards. The top hand is doing the work by pulling inwards and levering off the gunwale. It is very much a jerk outwards. The blade does not go out far; too much and the canoe stalls. (If you need more and immediate steering you pump the pry element: allow the blade to be carried back to the hull by the current and then jerk the pry a second time.) Finish by returning to the power stroke.

The stern pry and the short J: the pry has the more powerful steering element but the short J is quicker. With the pry, after the power phase you let go of the water before bringing the blade up on edge to steer. There is a moment of hesitation that creates a staccato action. The pry allows us to lean away from the stroke, which can be crucial in whitewater. The J locks us to the paddling side. In normal travel, I will constantly use the short J, it is easier on the body and more fluent. In whitewater, I use a mixture of these strokes as appropriate.

Many have described the C stroke as a bow draw followed by a power stroke and then a J. It is not. That combination is powerful and one I use in shallow water to lessen the trip hazard, but it misses the point. The C is a continuous movement rather than the staccato of the draw, power and J combination. Both have their place but they are very different; once you get the fluency of the C you will love it.

The **C stroke** is an elegant and efficient stroke with two uses. From stationary, we can use a single C stroke to get going in a straight line before continuing with a J. The second use (shown here) is to keep power through an arcing turn.

The start of the sequence is really an extended bow rudder position. The paddle blade describes an arc through the water, with the blade following a track that takes it below the canoe. By keeping pressure on the same face throughout the move, the blade reappears at the back of the canoe in a J position; the indicator thumb is down. Note the lovely curve of water behind the canoe. To continue the curving track you can repeat the stroke.

You can add to this in various ways. You can start with a bow rudder and, as it slows, sweep in with a C. At the end of the C you could slice the blade forwards as in the recovery phase of the Indian Stroke. I often use this on whitewater when making eddy turns (although I have to be convinced there is enough water under the canoe; meeting a rock with the blade can be quite a damp experience).

A cross-deck hanging draw using the slower water to one side.

Going Sideways on the Move

The ability to move the boat sideways while it is moving forwards is a very important skill which can get you out of difficult situations. Just as an example, it is often easier to miss an obstacle by moving the boat a short distance sideways, rather than trying to turn and ending up broached on the rock you were trying to avoid.

Errol has never done this before so he is set up with the paddle in position. Lina will then give him a push forwards. Errol gently rotates the blade to side-slip. As an alternative, you can pull the canoeist towards you on a rope.

To perform a **hanging draw**, the canoe needs forward speed. In the first photo the blade is in the draw position with the indicator thumb pointing to the stern. Chest and knees are rotated to the paddling side. The blade is then put in parallel to the direction of travel and level with your hip. The power face of the blade is towards the canoe and the indicator thumb is pointed backwards. After a split second you gently rotate the leading edge of the blade away from the canoe. This allows water to hit the inside face of the blade, providing a strong pulling action. The canoe side-slips to its right (the paddle side).

There is rarely a perfect spot for the paddle and, as the canoe side-slips, it often starts to turn. If the canoe turns to the paddle side then close the angle of the blade so that it is slicing parallel to the boat and then move the paddle back and reopen. If it turns away from the paddle side, move the blade forwards.

The hanging draw can be done across the deck (***cross-deck hanging draw***). As the paddle swings across, slide your knees to face the off-side. The power face of the blade is towards the canoe and the indicator thumb points forward. The blade should be put in parallel to the centreline and then gradually opened until pressure is felt. The blade goes into the water level to where it would be in the hanging draw on the opposite side; you can use a rivet, your body or a piece of tape as a marker.

The ***running pry*** is a dynamic method of side-slipping your canoe away from your paddle side. If you have mastered the hanging draw, this is just the opposite. Instead of the leading edge of the blade being angled away from the canoe, it is angled towards it. The shaft is on the side of the canoe so there is no pressure on you. The boat has forward momentum. The blade is slashed in from behind and the side. As the blade is angled then the moment the paddle connects with the hull it will kick the canoe sideways away from the paddle side.

I use this as an emergency avoidance stroke. Slam the running pry in as far forwards as possible, kicking the bow away from the paddling side. Then allow the paddle to be slid back along the gunwale to push the rest of the canoe away from the obstruction.

It is sometimes difficult to know how well these manoeuvres are going, so try parallel parking at a jetty or use buoys to gauge your success.

When **_side-slipping a tandem canoe_**, the idea is to go from travelling forwards in a straight line to travelling forwards and sideways. It is satisfying and slick when done well. A number of different strokes are combined, the action of the bow paddler being matched by the stern.

The canoe has forward speed and the bow paddler does a hanging draw. As the bow begins to move sideways, a stern rudder is used to cause the stern to follow suit. The bow leads the move. If the bow points away from the move, it will cause the side-slip to stall.

[1] A cross-deck hanging draw at the bow is matched by a hanging draw at the stern. Note the amount of chest rotation used to get strong positions for the arms.

[2] A bow jam paired with a hanging draw.

Reversing

There are a number of strokes which we use to go backwards for short distances, stop or slow the canoe. In river running, being able to slow the canoe down buys you time to scout the rapid from the boat and allows you to position your boat by reverse ferry gliding.

The cross-deck reverse is a powerful way of applying reverse power for the solo paddler. The paddler has moved forwards in the canoe to un-weight the stern. This makes it easier to steer as otherwise the stern would be deep in the water, tending to plough off course. For the on-side stroke, place the blade in behind the hips and drive the paddle forwards. Use the back face to push against the water. Without swapping hands, do a cross-deck stroke. The knees are shifted slightly to point towards the off-side, allowing the body to rotate more easily. The chest is turned strongly to the off-side. The power face of the blade is facing forwards and the indicator thumb on the top hand is pointing out. The blade is pulled towards the front of the canoe. The paddle is then switched back to the on-side.

Setting into an eddy, both paddlers are using reverse paddling to slow and angle into the slow water downstream of the rocks. The canoes are stern heavy, so steering has to be positive to control the angle of the canoe. It is not practical to change the boat trim in such a dynamic and fast environment.

In a tandem crew, the bow paddler uses a reverse J while the stern paddler uses a reverse power stroke. Note how he has slid forward off his seat to lighten the stern.

Using the **reverse J** we can go backwards and steer without swapping sides. The boat is trimmed bow heavy to ease the backwards steering. The stroke starts behind you and the paddle is pushed forwards. As the blade passes between your hip and knee, the paddle shaft starts running along the gunwale. The top hand and indicator thumb rotate downwards, causing the blade to turn outwards and start the steering. The indicator thumb is down. The paddle is levered off the gunwale, providing a powerful steering element.

A **compound backwater stroke** is a powerful way of slowing or reversing a canoe. The paddler is reversing his canoe. He has reached for the stern of the canoe with his paddle. There is rotation of the chest to the paddling side. The power face of the blade is facing the front of the canoe and his indicator thumb is pointing inwards. The blade is drawn back towards the hip. Just before the hip he quickly rotates the paddle so that the indicator thumb points out and the power face of the blade faces the stern. A normal backwater stroke is done, finishing with a reverse J.

Support Strokes

Staying upright is mainly about shifting your weight to stay in balance. However, if the water throws you off balance, you are going to need some help from the paddle. The **_low support_** is the stroke you need if you are falling towards the paddle. The aim is to get the weight back inside the gunwales and use that shift to right the canoe.

As you go off balance, the chest is turned towards the water and the arms are in a brace position with knuckles on both hands and the back of the blade towards the water. As the paddle hits the water, both hands are outside the gunwale. With the lower legs or ankles hooked under the seat thwart, you are still part of the canoe. The blade is supported briefly and, at that moment, your weight, chest and face are all turned towards the water. When the downwards momentum is stopped, the paddle is no longer important. Your head travels low across the canoe and is tucked down into the opposite side. Keep the head down for a moment to let the canoe steady, and then sit up.

In easier situations the use of the blade on the water and the shift of weight from one knee to the other will be sufficient. The blade is either twisted and sliced back to the surface or it can be sliced forwards giving support on the way.

Do not confuse this vertical support stroke with the horizontal high support in kayak. The chest is turned to the stroke side and there is no stress on the shoulder joints. In most ways it is a draw stroke as shown early but now used for support.

The **high support** is the solution if you are falling away from the paddle. The paddler has already started to fall to his right. With the paddle on his left he performs a draw stroke. Not much of the blade is in the water; with slightly more lean on the boat it would be time for a swim. The draw works and this enables the paddler to keep his weight within the gunwales: success. This is always a marginal stroke, however; although it has kept him in the boat, it's not as powerful as the low support.

By combining the high and low support as a tandem crew, you are in with a chance.
If it doesn't work, you have someone else to blame.

Paul is making a last desperate and successful effort to prevent a capsize to his right. His high support becomes static using the power of the flow beneath the wave.

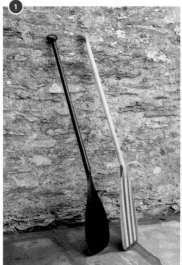

[1] The left paddle is of graphite and weighs only 10oz, some 280 grams, half the weight of the wood version. The power face of the blade is showing.

[2] We no nah Minnesota II, The canoe is lightweight (made of Kevlar) with a sharp entry.

[3] A Kevlar Jenson 18, travelling fast on flat water.

Bent Paddles and Fast Boats

If you are paddling flat water a fast boat and bent paddles (elbow paddles) make a superb and efficient combination. Once you have used them for a long trip it's hard to revert to a straight shaft.

The bend in the paddleshaft pitches the top hand further forward so we can use both hands for the drive of the blade. Most of the time you use a stroke very similar to that with a straight paddle. To go quickly, shorten the stroke and clip it out at the hip, the blade slices out at ninety degrees to the canoe.

Sit and switch (Minnesota switch) originated as a marathon racing technique but it has a place with recreational canoeists. Competition paddlers will switch sides every twelve to eighteen strokes. Each side of the body gets a work out. For the recreational paddler the switch may be done at the same interval, particularly at the start of the day when warming up or heading into a wind. Once into our day we may not swap so often, maybe every twenty minutes.

The bow paddler's stoke is parallel to the centre line of the canoe.

At the end of the stroke the paddle is lifted and the top hand released. The top hand is re-placed on the shaft below the bottom hand. What was the bottom hand slides up to the grip. The 'new' bottom hand moves up slightly. Barely a moment lost they are up and running on the opposite sides.

Timing the switch; the stern paddler can call the swap to suit their steering. A call of 'hut' is made to time the swap. Call 'hut' during one stroke, do one more and then swap. Some racers call 'hut' at the start of a stroke and swap at the end. Working hard the 'hut' is only a grunt as you exhale. If you have the breath to say 'bungalow' or anything else you are not working hard enough!

Rivers

❝ *Alex's skill with the paddle was superb and he manoeuvred his canoe with real ease on flat water. He was able to easily and accurately describe paddlers' performances from DVDs in detail; however, this was not enough to make him a skilled moving water paddler.*

I watched him with interest as we begun his transformation. I put him into easy rapids and set him moves across the current. He was disjointed and had no flow to his manoeuvres.

I worked on changing the angles of the boat in the moving water, and his fluency increased. Many moves on different rapids were tried out. We looked at the water during each move, and he was shown how to read what the impact of the water would be on the canoe and its line of travel. As he increased his understanding and proficiency, he learnt how this could be used to initiate moves.

The last rapid of the day was to be paddled: there was a small eddy in the middle of the river between two power jets of current. I ran the rapid to demonstrate the angle, speed and the use of the water to gain the mid-river eddy.

I walked back up to join Alex. His immediate and automatic response was to ask me about the paddle strokes. I simply directed him to run through the speed and angle of the boat.

'But what strokes?' was his reaction.

'Forget the strokes', I told him. 'You are good enough, they will just happen. Concentrate on speed and angle. It's about putting the boat in the right place so that it wants to do the move.'

This was to be the breakthrough run for Alex. For the first time his focus and concentration was totally on the right things. His boat was at the right speed and angle and he was using he water. He made the move look easy. He went from strength to strength through the next days, looking as fluent and confident on whitewater as he was on the flat.

It is not about the paddle. It is easy to be focused on strokes and miss the essentials of whitewater paddling. We need to concern ourselves with speed, angles and edge rather than the paddle. Differences in water can be utilised to change our direction. If we get these things right, the canoe will want to do the move and we will not be fighting the water.

Safety

Safety is based on knowledge and experience. Experience needs to be built up gradually so your first whitewater trips are best made with experienced companions, or enrol on a course of instruction. If you are going to 'go for it' take things gently and start on easy rivers. Hazards that are easily avoided by the experienced can be death traps for the unwary.

Are you prepared for a swim and can you retrieve your boat and kit afterwards? Low water and warm conditions will make things safer. Ask yourself plenty of 'what-if's. It is not necessarily about avoiding risk, but understanding it and making decisions.

Those that have paddled for years understand that even rivers they know can change. Boulders can move, trees can block the river around the bend or in high water a previously easy drop may have a recirculating stopper at its base. It takes time to build the experience to know when to show caution.

Can you cope with a swim in the conditions you will encounter?

Water does not always travel in straight lines.

Water Features

Understanding how whitewater behaves and being able to read the river is a vital skill. Water does not always travel in straight lines[1]. In the photo above, a shingle bank on river left is deflecting the main flow around to river right close into the bank.

Constrictions may force the current in towards the centre of the river, concentrating power and volume. The flow forms a distinctive V pointing in the downstream direction[2]. The paddler is running a ***downstream V*** and having great fun[3]. The standing waves are caused by the concentration of water and conceal no rocks.

The last photo shows the same type of standing waves, but the Bloodvein is in massive ***flood***[4]. It is not runnable in a canoe and most kayakers would think twice. The water is so powerful that massive boils are forming to the side of the main flow and eddies are running back upstream at speed. Flood conditions can turn a normally easy river into an extremely dangerous place to be.

A small surface wave indicates the presence of a hidden rock upstream.

A patch of slow water indicating a rock upstream.

In high water, this normally sedate eddy has become a seething cauldron of whirlpools and boils.

Where an obstruction sticks out into the current, an **_eddy_** is formed downstream[1]. This eddy has a gentle current running back upstream. Eddies may be gentle affairs with still water or can recirculate at any speed up to that of the main current. In more difficult sections, we will use eddies like the climber uses a ledge; they give us time to recover and look at the route ahead.

Planning the Line

It is easy to focus on the biggest feature or the difficult section in a rapid. Once I have sorted the 'crux' of a rapid, I will carefully look at the water upstream. Where is the current running at the start? If I get the start right and read the water well, then the hard bit may be easy.

Try to choose markers so you have intermediate targets before hitting the more difficult section. I often explain this as 'joining the dots'. It helps to plan and visualise a route in our heads before running it.

You will see many examples of using these markers in subsequent sections.

On the Chassezac a paddler commits to a bend with confidence. He had landed for a look prior to running it. With the increased height he could see into the channel; it was clear and he could see onto easier water and eddies beyond.

River Hazards

▐▐ *With the river high we set off cautiously. We came to the section that gave me concern. The river was wide and running around a very long right-hand bend. On the outside was a vertical earth bank and on the inside slower water and a beach. An inexperienced paddler could get swept to the outside of the bend and we could not see the whole way around this. If the group had not been coping, I would have lined the canoes down on rope.*

However, the group had no problem keeping to the slow water on the inside of the bend. But my caution had been justified; at the end of the bend there was a jammed tree stump. All the strong flow on the outside of the bend hit this obstruction. We paddled past with ease on the inside.

I learned later that a kayak group had come unstuck. The quality of leadership was poor and several of the group were swept onto the tree. One person had their legs broken when the kayak folded around the tree, but thankfully no one lost their life. The bend was no more than Grade 1 water, just very fast. **▐▐**

If you can't manoeuvre so as to see around the bend, get out and look!

The metal structure is a bridge. There is a wire fence completely hidden.

This cattle fence will be an invisible hazard in high water.

If the river is wide and the current slow I can meander around **bends** with an easy mind. If there is a problem I can easily manoeuvre or paddle back upstream. If the current is stronger and I could not paddle against it, I must show caution. Around that corner there may be a tree blocking the outside of the bend or even the whole river. Is there a harder rapid or even a weir?

Strainers are anything that will let the water through but will stop a boat or swimmer. Twice I have seen people swim through strainers (not members of my group, I add) and it is a terrifying sight. On both occasions the individual was lucky but there was little we could have done to help if they had not reappeared. The web of branches might stop a swimmer or a branch may snag equipment and hold them under.

The only way to deal with strainers is to avoid them. Make every effort not to be swept into a strainer whether paddling or swimming. In the worst-case swimming scenario, the normal advice is to face down-river and swim at the obstruction at speed. Try and launch yourself over or into the branches and not be swept under.

The outwash plain at the end of the River Spey. As the river widens it drops rocks and gravel, and its ability to carry trees diminishes. The channel often changes; the water can be fast and there are always new tree blockages.

This tree has been washed from the bank and is only slowly starting its journey downstream. The first time I paddle past this spot with the tree missing, I am going to wonder where it is lying in wait.

If you are going to be swept under branches, then get low. Do not grab the branches, as the boat will continue, dumping you in the river. With luck and a few scratches, you emerge on the other side.

Trees often hook up on bridges. The right-hand arch is totally blocked, but I have seen it when the centre was blocked.

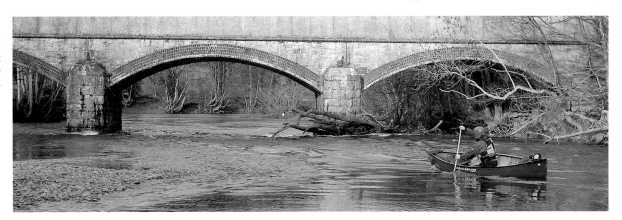

Stoppers (hydraulics) are formed when natural ledges cause water to speed up as it drops over. This then leaves a low point in the river and the surface water rushes back upstream to fill the gap. This water boils to the surface and pours upstream as a mass of white before tumbling into the low point and being swept down again.

A swimmer or canoe can be held in the water below the drop which is being re-circulated. In this case, the swimmer is eventually kicked clear but it may need a rescue. In the situation shown below Lina was standing by with a throw line, just in case. In other situations, a rescuer wearing a specialist harness on a buoyancy aid may have to go into the stopper after the swimmer; this puts the rescuer at risk and requires specialist training.

Weirs (or low head dams) are built for a variety of purposes. The weir in the photo above extracts water to feed a canal; alternative uses may be for irrigation purposes or to provide deep water for navigation. In the past, a weir may have driven a water wheel. Stoppers formed by weirs often lack a weakness or outwash and will hold a swimmer. If in doubt, assume that a stopper formed by a weir is dangerous and portage.

There is an 'event horizon' in the river. We can see the line and flat water in the distance but not what happens between.

The same weir seen from below. The big wave in the centre is runnable but the canoe would probably swamp. Further out, the recirculation is very powerful and a canoe would be stopped, swept backwards and held.

The same weir in low water. The tow back into the weir face from below is still powerful and it would be likely to hold a swimmer. The ramp in the middle is a canoe shoot. Weirs that can be perfectly safe at one water level can be dangerous at another.

This river-wide weir is absolutely lethal. The tow back is long and a swimmer would be constantly re-circulated. Rescue would be impossible.

The canoe may crash through this violent wave, but would almost certainly swamp and capsize. A swimmer would be swept under the wave and downstream.

A measuring weir. The far side of the weir has a massive recirculation and is lethal. This side of the central obstruction has a possible route where the recirculation is less strong, but we decided not to chance our luck and portaged.

Some weirs have canoe shoots: these can be great fun and save portaging.

Campsite on the Rio Grande.

You usually have notice of **rising water**. Most times it will be obvious that bad weather is affecting things; in this case move camp and boats higher (I often tie the canoes as an extra precaution). A river may become considerably more difficult as rapids become bigger and longer.

On wilderness journeys, the catchment area of a river can be huge. Storms may occur hundreds of kilometres away from where you are paddling, so it may not be apparent that a storm surge is coming.

Camping in one of the canyons of the Rio Grande we heard a distant thunderstorm. We moved tent, kit and canoe higher in case of flash flooding (hard work after a long day). With rising water you do not want to be trapped with a cliff or channel behind you, so have an upward escape route. The river did not rise, but I slept easy.

For more on river features and hazards see *Whitewater Safety and Rescue* by Franco Ferrero.

Guide Books & Grading

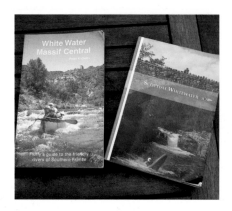

There are river guides for many regions of the world. They describe the grade, access and egress and details of the rapids. You can have a whole book either devoted to a single river or with information on the rivers of a region or the rivers of an entire country.

Some guides, particularly for wilderness areas, may be canoe specific; others will be written from a kayak perspective. What may be an easy set of waves for a kayak may swamp a canoe.

There is an **_International grading system_** consistent from country to country. Grades do vary according to water level, however; what might be classed as a grade 2 under normal conditions may become much harder in higher water.

Grade 1	These are small rapids with easily avoided obstructions. The waves are regular.
Grade 2	The stream and waves are irregular. There could be small stoppers, eddies and whirlpools. There can be simple obstructions and small drops.
Grade 3	High irregular waves. Larger rapids with stoppers, eddies and whirlpools. There could be isolated boulders obstructing the stream, small drops and multiple obstructions. In a canoe we may need to get out and inspect this grade of rapid, but there should be a recognisable route.
Grade 4	The route may not be recognisable from the boat so a bank inspection is necessary. A traditional canoe is generally out of place on this grade of water. There will be heavy continuous rapids, stoppers and whirlpools. There are likely to be boulders obstructing the flow with undertow.
Grade 5	The route is difficult to recognise and inspection essential. These are extreme rapids with narrow passages, steep drops and powerful water features. This is the province of the very best C1 and OC1 boaters.

1 Grade 3 on the Bonnet Plume in Canada's North West.

2 Grade 2 on the River Ardèche in France.

3 Bala Mill Falls on the Tryweryn is probably a soft-touch grade 4.

4 Linn of Tummel in high water, grade 5.

5 Grade 1 on the River Dee in North Wales.

Jamie and Alun are in deep discussion as they plan their move across the river.

On some inspections you should wear helmets. The people in the above photo made their own choice as it was easy terrain. Everyone put their helmets on to run the rapid.

River running techniques

Teamwork is essential. We need to agree on what we are going to do. Shouting at each other in the middle of a rapid is rarely productive. We need to have clear strategies for river running and plans for individual rapids.

When the line is not obvious you may need to make an *inspection*. Each paddler or tandem team needs to agree a line and have marks they can use on the water to follow it.

Dave Luke (a coach based in North Wales) has an interesting series of questions he gets clients to ask themselves when they are inspecting a rapid:

- Where does the flow take you if you don't paddle?

- What are the hazards?

- What is the line down the rapid that avoids the hazards and uses the flow?

- What are the consequences of blowing your line?

- If the flow takes you towards a hazard what manoeuvres do you need to do to avoid it and stay on line?

- Do you have the skill to perform those manoeuvres?

- Are you going to run the rapid, line it, or portage?

Whether we are in solo or tandem canoes, you need to focus on where you want the canoe to be and not on something you wish to miss: *make positive moves not negative ones*. If we concentrate on a rock or tree we wish to miss then we are more likely to hit it.

If our eyes, head and chest are pointing to the place we wish to be, then we maximise our focus and the chance of getting there. The paddler's aim is clear. He is heading for the peak of the wave just left of the white wave.

You will often start your journey down a river from an eddy, and then go in and out of them as you progress downstream. Leaving an eddy involves **breaking into the current** with forward speed.

In the sequence below, the paddlers approach the eddy line at a suitable angle of around 45 degrees. Just before the eddy line, they put more weight onto their left knees to edge the canoe to the left. This is the direction in which the water is going to turn the canoe. The stern is in the slow water of the eddy and the bow is about to enter the current. With the bow in the current and the boat edged to the left it is being pushed into its turn. The turn complete, both are paddling forwards. For a quicker turn, the bow paddler could have done a cross-bow rudder.

CURRENT

Experiment with the angle and speed at which you need to hit the eddy line on an easy set of eddies. These factors will have a massive impact on where the boat goes next and the speed of the turn. Beyond this, try crossing the eddy line with a target already agreed or located downstream. All of this will equip you with the necessary skills for river running.

This pair are approaching the eddy line more dynamically. The boat is edged just before crossing the eddy line and the stern paddler is doing a sweep to quicken the turn. As they transit into the flow, the bow paddler uses a bow rudder to tighten the turn. Both paddlers are intent on where they are aiming.

Although breaking in is primarily about angle and speed, in the last two photos above you can see how a bow rudder can help the turn. The paddlers have powered up the eddy. The canoe is well edged and the bow paddler is in a dynamic and powerful position to pull the bow around. There is little angle on the blade but the force is still huge. There is nothing the stern paddler can do other than help lean the canoe. Keeping the acceleration up, she has drawn her bow rudder in and is now turning it into a power stroke. As the canoe flattens, her partner will be able to paddle again.

To get back into an eddy you will need to be able to **break out of the current**. With a good angle and forward speed, the paddlers are heading for the eddy line. As they cross the eddy line they are already edged towards the direction of turn. The eddy is large so they don't really need a tight turn; they do no strokes and allow the water to pull the canoe around to face upstream.

In the above sequence, the paddler wants to perform a tight turn so he is tight to the top of the eddy. Using a lot of edge and a powerful bow rudder, he pivots tightly just inside the eddy line.

Where you want to end up in an eddy will depend on a number of factors. It may be a small eddy, so you need to be tight to the top and turn close to the eddy line. The eddy may be big and have its own current re-circulating upstream, in which case you may enter it low down and ride the current back up.

An eddy turn is being gained with a cross-bow rudder.

On easy eddies, experiment with different angles of approach. Vary your speed and try to end up at different points in the eddy. Try using different stroke combinations. All this will allow you to learn how to apply the technique in a variety of different situations, in other words skilfully. Do this with both breaking and breaking out.

The paddlers in the above sequence were only on their 4th-ever day of paddling. The boats were laden with kit for an overnighter in the Ardèche Gorge. They made a good diagonal approach with speed and commitment. The angle was perfect and the bow paddler had a good bow rudder to anchor the turn. However, the canoe is flat and should have had a strong lean into the turn. The canoe piled into water on the outside of the turn, and there was nothing the stern paddler could do. Capsize was inevitable. It had been an awesome attempt with just the edge missing. They pulled the boat back upstream for a second go and got it absolutely right.

Approaching the main drop, the bow paddler is using a cross-bow draw to straighten the canoe. On reaching the end of the rapid, the bow paddler changes to a powerful bow rudder/hanging draw to turn the canoe towards the eddy.

Traditionally, the more experienced paddler goes in the stern of a tandem. In white-water, however, it is hard to overstress the **importance of the bow paddler**. Once you are underway there is little time for communication and the noise makes instruction from the back unclear. In many ways, the stern is following the bow paddler down the rapid and relies on their eyes.

Good bow paddlers are a delight to paddle behind. Treat them well. Make sure you both understand the line and, where necessary, defer to the bow. Do not shout at them. If they are inexperienced, get out of the habit of telling them when to do strokes; both of you will have a far more enjoyable time.

Robin was too used to being told when to time his strokes. I needed to cure him of this. We had agreed the line down a powerful piece of water and headed for an eddy. As we entered it, Robin swung his paddle across the boat and hung it in the air ready for the necessary cross-bow rudder. I kept silent. With his paddle still in the air the canoe ploughed its way up the beach at the back of the eddy.

After a shocked silence I quietly explained that he was experienced enough and he could make his own decisions as to when to turn. Tough love can be effective and, within an eddy or two, we were operating smoothly.

River right and river left refer to the direction when facing downstream.

There are many different ways to break-out and many combinations of strokes that can be used. The photos above illustrate a **low brace/cross-bow rudder** combination. The bow paddler is using a powerful cross-deck bow rudder (a little too far forward). The stern paddler is using a low brace for stability. The weight is on their left knees and the edge is extreme. Water is spilling into the canoe, but without that much edge they would capsize to their right. The low brace gives the reassurance to put the extreme edge on. Well into the eddy, the combination of angled approach and cross-bow rudder is pulling them through the eddy turn.

There are times when we will need to move across the current but without moving down the river. A **forward ferry glide** will achieve this. The ferry glide is done with the canoe and paddler facing upstream. The trim needs to be bow light as for all normal paddling.

The paddler has broken out into the eddy on river right[1]. Below is a bend and he is moving across the river to get a better viewpoint. He has built up speed in the eddy. Crossing from the slow current to the much faster main flow he has angled the boat to the right. The canoe is leant downstream. Without this lean, the current would capsize the canoe upstream. Forward power and the angle are maintained and the canoe heads across the river. (Sometimes you may choose to lose ground to achieve a specific objective.) He hits the eddy, and turns back upstream.

Having come across to river left it has been decided to ferry back across to the original bank. The paddler builds up speed in the eddy. (Many paddlers would swap sides so the paddle is on the downstream side.) The canoe is leant to the left (downstream). With the paddle on the upstream side you have a powerful corrective stern pry position, preventing the water turning the canoe downstream. With the paddle on this side it is vital that the canoe is leant the opposite way. Only part of the blade is used to steer. The angle of the canoe to the current is maintained along with forward power.

The paddler has too great an angle and is correcting this with a powerful stern sweep/draw. His top hand is punching outwards and the bottom arm is pulling in to turn the bow back upstream.

Having used the ferry to get a better view, the decision has been made to run the rapid close to the right bank.

In the case of **tandem ferries**, bow paddlers can help with the angle but their primary role is to provide power. If the bow paddler is paddling on the downstream side, they must be wary of using a cross-bow stroke to correct the angle as it is easy to put weight on the upstream side. This could easily result in a capsize and a miffed stern swimmer.

The **reverse ferry** works well as a method of manoeuvring. It is defensive in that it slows the boat, allowing time for the bow to rise over waves. It is a good way of keeping to the inside of a corner or avoiding a wave train.

In the sequence below, the boat is heading downstream under forward power. The paddlers want to reverse ferry out to their left, but the canoe is angled the wrong way. The bow paddler is pulling the bow right with a cross-bow draw and the stern paddler is using a reverse sweep to push the stern left. Once the angle is correct, they both apply reverse power. Both paddlers work to maintain the angle but need

to be quick about this, as the move requires powerful reverse stokes. With a good angle and reverse power, the canoe is slowed; they move to the left clear of the wave train. They can now head forwards again.

In the sequence below, a reverse ferry is being used to keep to the inside of the bend. The river is very fast and yet another sharp bend is ahead. The paddler is paddling defensively and this enables him to stay in slightly slower water and take the opportunity to set into the eddy at the end of the section. The keys to success are a good angle and steady application of reverse power. Doing this, the water will press on the outside (in relation to the bend) of the canoe, helping to keep you close to the inside of the bend. Any steering strokes are done at the front of the canoe: reverse J, bow draw and cross-bow draw are all effective. Even if it feels that it is the stern being dragged around, the bow is the only effective area in which to correct things. He finishes the manoeuvre off with massive reverse strokes to set into the eddy.

In the previous photos the canoes were stern heavy since this is the trim you need most of the time on the river; situations arise too quickly to change trim e.g. before doing a reverse ferry. This actually makes the manoeuvre more difficult as the water can grab the stern and prevent us setting or changing an angle. However, a bold approach works wonders: set a good angle from the first moment and it generally goes well. If you need to change the angle, particularly if the stern feels 'stuck', do a couple of quick, decisive forward stokes (going forward frees the stern) and then immediately reset the angle.

Lina is demonstrating an easy way to practise the manoeuvre. The current is easy but consistent. She has moved forwards in the canoe to free the stern and allow the current to slide below it. Steering at the stern will now work, but she is practising steering at the bow so when she does this with a stern-heavy boat she will have the right skills.

When **setting into an eddy** you need to ensure that you have very little angle to the current. Slow the canoe with a combination of on-side and cross-deck strokes. Once your stern is clear of the rock that forms the eddy, apply massive reverse on the outside of the move (it is best to have the paddle on the outside of the move). When the stern is in the eddy, the rest of the canoe will follow. It is important to get the stern in first. If the bow goes in first then the current will grab the stern and spin the canoe. In tandem, the bow paddler must resist the temptation to pull the bow into the eddy before the stern.

Setting into an eddy.

This is a 'must-make eddy' on a narrow creek. To ensure the manoeuvre, one of the group is using his paddle as an 'arrester hook'.

The paddler has set into the eddy. Once across the eddy line she uses a far-back stroke to anchor the canoe into the eddy. The stroke can be pulled forwards and then sliced back for a second pull. She is using the power face of the blade.

I have seen two of my friends swamp here in much bigger water. They got over the first wave before plunging steeply into the next pyramid of a wave. Swamped, they managed to get to within feet of the shore before capsizing.

A cross-bow rudder has been moved back to almost a cross-deck hanging draw position. This enables the canoe to **carve through the turn** and open up the arc. At the end, the blade can be moved forwards to retighten the turn.

Sometimes **avoiding waves** is the best policy. It can be great fun running a downstream V: the sheer amount of water colliding and forcing its way into the centre creates a series of standing waves. As the volume increases, so does the size of the standing waves.

You may wish to miss the centre of the V. Paddle diagonally across the current aiming for the sidewall of the first waves[1]. The move depends on aggressive forward speed, allowing you to punch directly into the eddy.

When expeditioning on steeper and bigger volume rivers *spraydecks* become useful. They allow you to run bigger waves and sustained rapids without taking on water. The spraydeck in attached to the boat by a series of hooks and elasticised loops. Each deck is made for a specific boat so the cockpit holes correspond to the seats beneath. The paddler fits into a sleeve that tightens around the waist. In the event of a capsize, the spraydeck stays attached to the canoe and the paddler exits the sleeve. Real care must be taken to keep the area around the paddler's feet clear of ropes and straps to ensure there is little risk of entrapment. They also work well in cold wet conditions keeping out rain and keeping the boat far drier.

Rapid on the Bonnet Plume, spraydeck essential!

The leader has jumped out and run down to the next obstacle. She does not get them to look but calls them through with a very clear signal as to the route. The paddlers skim through the edge of the stopper and head on to the next eddy.

River right and river left refer to the direction when facing downstream.

Making positive moves. Good paddlers use boat angle and speed, and anticipate the effect of different areas of water to achieve moves and lines.

" *This bend in the Guil (France) created a problem. Water was piling into the **river left** bank, forming a powerful jet of water and standing waves which cut diagonally across and straight at the trees on river right. There were tangled roots and debris providing a real possibility of a fatal pin. The problem was apparent from upstream so we eddied out and walked down for a closer look. Lina was running the rapid with a clear plan.*

Lina paddled a line that was strongly angled across the current. She was aiming to cut across the jet and hit the slower water on river left. All of Lina's attention was on the jet and the eddy beyond it. She was making a positive move not a negative one; she looked at where she was going and not what she was avoiding.

The jet has pushed the nose downstream. This was anticipated, however, and the angle was set to allow for this; the canoe continued to cut across the jet.

The bow of the canoe entered the slower water and the canoe effectively made an eddy turn. Lina was not close enough to the top of the eddy to stay in place, but the slower water was pulling her away from the jet and the obstruction. **"**

S turns link two eddy turns into a smooth continuous whole. It is an elegant and effective way of crossing a jet. Having the paddle on the downstream side gives stability during the first turn. Speed is built up in the eddy. Edging to the right is natural because that is the paddle side. The canoe has forward speed and is edged right. If the water was moving any faster, you would do a low brace on the water rather than hold the paddle ready for use in the air. The bow has entered the slow water and the canoe is still edged right; edge left too soon and its swim time. Just as your knees are about to cross the eddy line, begin to gently transfer the weight to the left knee. Once the weight is on your left knee and the canoe is heavily edged to the left, a cross-bow rudder tightens the turn.

We can also do the converse and cross through an eddy in the centre of the river by S turning from the current, through the eddy and back into the current.

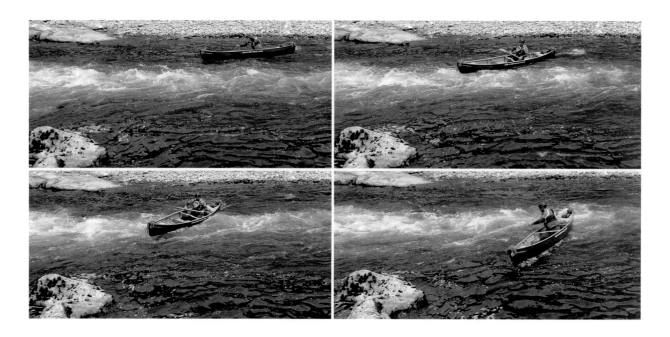

When paddling tandem, you must have a clear and agreed understanding. The stern paddler could be doing a low brace for stability, and just after the bow paddler enters the eddy the boat is rolled gently to the right. Changing the edge too soon or late could lead to a capsize.

It is a good test of skill and understanding to practise this move with the paddle on the upstream side. By building up speed in the eddy, the canoe edges to the paddling side: this is the wrong edge for crossing the eddy line. Just before crossing the eddy line the edge is changed to lean downstream. Edge is maintained downstream with it being rolled the other way as your knees enter the eddy.

In the final photo, a stern rudder is used to turn to the right. The paddle angle is lower and the pressure is on the outer face of the blade. The blade is tilted slightly away from the boat.

Surfing is fun … and it enables us to switch from one bank to the other. Build up speed in the eddy, then cross the shoulder of the wave and enter the trough. Too little speed and you won't climb over and onto the wave. Too much and you climb onto the wave above, lose speed and get pushed off downstream. It is easier with the paddle on the outside of the move. As the boat slides on, it will attempt to turn left. You can use the powerful stern rudder to turn the nose back to the right.

Coming onto the wave with the paddle on the inside of the move is much harder. As you slide onto the wave, the canoe is going to try to make a diagonal run to the right. The third photo in the sequence shows a stern hanging draw used to pull the stern to the right and turn the bow to the left. The leading edge of the blade is angled slightly away from the boat, so that the water is hitting it on the inside. This creates a pull away from the canoe. Lean back to push the blade further back. The top arm is pushed out and away from the boat and the bottom arm is cranked in.

Learning the steering strokes on all but the easiest waves is hard. Everything happens so quickly. Standing in the water[1], Lina can get her student to mimic the stroke or can adjust the angles for them. We can practise in a boat while being held by a rope[2]. This does not need a wave but just a decent flow and a river shallow enough to stand safely. It does not even need to be a big wave to learn on[3]. In this case, the entry was slightly awkward so Keiron was sliding the canoes onto the wave.

Crossing the river on waves saves energy and can be very stylish. In the rapid shown below it would have been easy to cross below the whitewater, but that will not always be a possibility. It is good to practise where the only consequences of failure are a wetting and the derision of the photographer.

Speed is built up and the canoe is edged as it slides onto the face of the wave. Edged to the downstream side, the canoe slides across the face of the wave (and it is fast, very fast). The stability comes from the speed and edge. No edge and the canoe will capsize upstream with gusto. If more stability was needed, the bow paddle could be on the water as a brace. As they hit the eddy on the far side, the paddlers roll the canoe's edge to the left. The bow paddler does a cross-deck draw to hold the bow and the stern paddler a low brace for stability.

Black Tooth

❚❚ *This is one of the few dangerous rapids in the Ardèche Gorge and, unfortunately for these two novices, the line on the rapid is not easy to achieve. The river sweeps around to its right, and the problem is the two rocks near the bottom of the rapid.*

The smaller rock creates an upstream pointing V of slower water. The bow of the novices' boat has cut into this. The slower water has pulled the nose across the river while the stern, being in faster water, has begun to swing. The only chance now would be to accelerate, but the paddlers are mesmerised by the rock.

Broad-side on to the rock and even with the enclosed hull of the sit-on-top, the force of the current is enough to start it folding. Had the boat hit more side on it would have stuck in place, as the upstream side of the rock is square and slightly undercut. This could be extremely dangerous in a canoe, with the possibility of legs being trapped under a kneeling thwart or seat. Luckily, the boat washes off.

Dave and Whinge show how it should be done with the canoe angled to their right. The canoe glances off the edge of the V of slower water and is pushed onto the correct line, easily sliding past the second rock.

In the second photo, the water level is higher and the group inexperienced. Broadsiding the main rock would likely pin and fold the canoe. We set the canoes for lining, and quickly and easily moved past the obstructions.

When the river goes out of sight around **blind corners** we wonder what is next. Does the river suddenly get much harder? Can I paddle back against the current? Has a tree fallen and blocked the line? In the following sequence, the lead paddler has broken out. She now has time to think and plan.

On the outside corner of bend is an eddy. The lead paddler is confident that she can guarantee getting the eddy. Once at the eddy she could get onto the bank and clamber up if necessary. If you go to an eddy with no exit other than downstream, then you are committed to whatever is around the corner.

She focuses on the target eddy, makes the eddy and has a good look downstream. The way ahead is clear so she is gives the thumbs up. If she needs to convey more information she will use the river signals.

To maintain **line of sight** around the corner, she could stay in the eddy and let the rest of the group go past her. She would then bring up the rear. They could 'eddy hop'. As the next paddler heads for her eddy, the lead paddler sets off downstream to the next eddy she can see. This process continues until everyone is down at a gathering eddy. She could wait in the eddy and call the others to her one by one. As each person gets to her they can look downstream, decided where they are going and leave Lina in the eddy to brief the next person. All of these methods should maintain the crucial line of sight around the bend.

We had spent some time inspecting and had decided to work down the rapid using three eddies. Decisions had to be correct as the Bloodvein River was high and the stoppers, in several places, were big enough to stop or swamp a boat. We were in agreement on where we were going over the first drop, so ran the canoe at an angle and speed into the first eddy on the right. At that stage a pause was used to confirm the next move, an S turn across the main current. This is a powerful move with lots of edge and speed; failure would result in being swept onto the rock wall lower down. We then slid down the left edge of the final drop and into the eddy below. An alternative, used by our other pair on this trip, was to paddle across the flat water above the rapid and portage the rapid on river left.

The second photo shows the river in a normal summer flow; the rock ledge we paddled over earlier is now a metre clear of the water and there is no strength in the current. Guidebooks can only give an indicator on lines and grades; much higher water levels make things more serious.

Left: rapid on Bloodvein River in high water. Right: same rapid in normal summer levels. Photo courtesy of Stuart Pollitt.

If you are signalling to someone in a rapid, do it early so they have plenty of time to see and react.

Whenever I paddle with new people I will go through signals. Check that everyone has the same understanding.

River Signals

Using a common set of signals enables paddlers to communicate simple information at a distance. The communication needs to be two-way. If you are at the other end of a signal then you can either repeat the signal, or nod. Repeating the signal for stop is particularly important. Check that everyone in your group has agreed on and is using the same signals.

Be wary of following the signals of a group that you have caught up on a river. They may not be following the same signals.

Here I am indicating the direction that the pair should head. Because they are only on their second day of paddling, I am inclining my body in the direction they should edge the canoe.

Some have an open hand and some a fist, but all mean 'one boat go'.

The same gesture but now pumped up and down means 'all boats go'. If you are receiving the signal then you still need to use common sense and space appropriately.

Stop! This is the signal I definitely like to see repeated. If I am using this signal there is inevitably something downstream that is serious.

This can be used to indicate assistance needed. I have seen it used by some groups as stop. See how confusion arises?

The hand and finger are describing a horizontal circle. It means 'catch an eddy', and is often followed by pointing at a particular eddy.

Only point where you want someone to go. Never point at dangers as others may think you are indicating the route. There have been fatalities because of this confusion.

Come to me! The hand is patted on the top of the head. Another sign to indicate one boat or all may follow. The leader is on the bank and can grab canoes as they arrive.

We can use the same signals, but extend them using the paddle. Although the signal is higher, it is not always more easily seen. Black against a dark environment is hard to see.

But let's not get too pedantic about this. A simple thumb up will often suffice.

Peel out at T-Ville . Photo courtesy of Harry Rock.

Lining, Tracking & Poling

It was the English Canoe Symposium and the main guest was Harry Rock, the American poling champion. I had been running workshops through the weekend and Sunday evening was my first chance to chat to Harry. He was very happy to discuss the merits of square stance poling but was certainly not dogmatic about it. For years I had used and taught a diagonal stance, so I looked forward to learning from and bouncing ideas with Mr Rock the next morning.

Ash and I were there early and got kitted up. Someone made rude comments about my lack of optimism in donning a drysuit. Ash and I were quickly on the water and, before the session proper started, we were attempting to climb the rapid and ledge above Brathay Pool. The route was awkward and even getting to the ledge was hard. The ledge stopped both of us and we were burning a lot of energy. The majority of the group were still on the bank, but Harry was now on the water.

With no fuss Harry headed upstream towards us. The awkward rapid now appeared straightforward for him, and his canoe climbed up and over the ledge with a fluent ease. Ash and I could only look on with envy. Harry said nothing but his body language was asking: "Ok boys, do you want some of this?"

Yes Mr Rock, we did!

The session he ran was outstanding and we were soon converted to the square stance. It was the most influential technical coaching I had received in years. I went home determined to take on the new style. It was a year and many swims later before I was back at Brathay Pool; I climbed the ledge at my first attempt. **"**

Set up

It is worth taking a little time to set up for lining and tracking. For harder situations, it is best to fit a **bridle** below the upstream end of the canoe. This means that the rope will not capsize the canoe.

In a separate length of rope some 3m long, an overhand knot is tied in the centre. The rope is laid across the canoe. The lining or tracking rope is attached to the bridle with, in this case, a bowline. The knot is under the centre of the canoe and the weight is at the downstream end. The ends of the bridle are fastened off to the seat (here with clove hitches but a round turn and two half-hitches also works).

A bridle can also be made from the main rope. Having sorted the length, she is tying an overhand knot in the bight of rope. The loop and the single strand are the same length. With the knot underneath, the loop will fasten to one side of the seat and the single strand to the other.

Lining

There are times when you do not want to run a rapid. Where possible you can avoid portaging by lining the canoe. This rapid shown below is straightforward except for a rock in the middle of the shoot. This is simple paddling for an intermediate paddler, but a great opportunity to introduce lining.

A bridle is fitted on the light end of the canoe and the load is at the opposite end of the boat. Take the rope in one hand and make a series of loops back and forth; these are known as lap or butterfly coils. The loops are kept small so that there is no chance of tripping yourself. There is no loop around your hand, so there is no chance of a coil tightening around it.

Taking in the spare rope using lap coils.

I often wear a helmet when lining as it is very easy to slip. On this day, the rocks were dry and the footing was good.

With the coils in one hand, the paddler prepares to push the canoe out. Concentration is on the feet with an occasional glance at the boat. The canoe is kept tight in on the corner and it slides through the gap. The canoe has run well clear of the rocks and a good pull on the rope sets the canoe into the eddy. If you are in strong current and have not used a bridle, this is the point where you can capsize the canoe. Finally, the canoe arrives safe and dry at the bank.

To get the canoe over a large drop or through a large stopper, the process can be reversed. The rope is pulled from the downstream side of the obstacle rather than held from above. The bridle is downstream and at the un-weighted end of the canoe. The upstream paddler releases the canoe and the downstream paddler pulls as fast as he can. The canoe is pulled through the corner of the stopper and into the eddy.

Lining is included in the art form that is canoeing. I have lined rapids that have been listed as portages. I have lined part of a rapid and run the rest. If the start of a portage is close to the top of a rapid, it may be safer to line to the final eddy. It pays to be creative and safe.

Avoiding a rapid on the Bloodvein. It is not always necessary to use a bridle and often, in simpler flows, I use the painter.

Tracking

There are occasions when you may wish to travel upstream. Maybe you have missed the get-out and need to go back, or you wish to cross a watershed and have to travel up one river to do so. Perhaps you just wish to make a challenging upstream journey. Which ever, it requires the ability to read water and make skilled judgements. If it's good enough for the salmon, we should give it a shot.

Moving upstream on the Durance. To avoid the powerful water, the canoes are tracked close inshore. All have a knife to hand.

Generally, the further away from the boat you are, the easier it is to get the tracking started. Kit is in the downstream end of the canoe and the bridle under the upstream lighter end. The trailing ends are kept knot-free. If you are using a throw bag then the bag will be at the boat, or removed. The second rope is attached to the stern at gunwale height. One bridle is generally enough but a bridle is needed at both ends with some canoes.

The paddler starts at a run, as you need to get the boat out into the fast water. If this is done slowly, the bow will be in faster water than the stern and the canoe will turn. Once the boat is out, you can concentrate on where you are walking.

In easy conditions there are shortcuts. The bow painter is looped through the seat and then under the canoe. There is no bridle but the pull is coming from under the boat. The stern rope is off the deck as usual.

Poling

Whenever the water is shallow poling gives us a practical way to make progress whether upstream or down. Where travel in shallow, mud-bottomed locations is common, people have come up with a number of adaptations to the simple pole. Feet are added to the end of the pole so that it doesn't sink into the mud. They can be as simple as curved pieces of twig lashed to the end of the pole, which splay out when pushed in, to purpose built feet.

In previous times, wooden **poles** were simply cut and shaped when and where needed. Most of us will use manufactured poles, however. Wood is nice and has an aesthetic quality. Generally wood poles are quite thick, to give strength, and there-fore do not sit as easily in the hand. A copper band added at each end stops the

It may be quicker to wade.

After a brutal portage I was glad to take to the water on the Carnoch.

wood from burring and splitting. A bolt can be screwed into the end and the top hack-sawed off to leave a spike of metal to grip the riverbed. Most manufactured poles are made from aluminium or glass fibre, however.

From bottom to top: a shop-bought split aluminium pole (the end cap is quite hard edged so there is a good grip on the riverbed); a fibreglass pole (the end cap is slightly rounded which means, unfortunately, it can lose grip on some surfaces); and two home-finished poles. In both cases a dowel of wood has been hammered into the end to seal it and enable it to float. One has had a bolt screwed into the end before the top was hack-sawed off. This metal spike gives a good grip on most river beds and is favoured by competition polers.

Split poles: one is made of fibreglass and the other aluminium. The tape on the glass pole shows that these are a pair. Because of the way the joint is manufactured, the holes do not necessarily match from pair to pair.

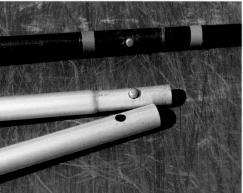

Glass fibre or kevlar poles are very convenient and light. They split in the middle so they are easily thrown into the car for transportation and stow easily in a canoe. Many of the poling sequences in the photographs show this type of pole. The inside is packed with foam and the ends capped. They tend to bend excessively under a dynamic push, and the end caps are slightly rounded so they do not get the best grip on the riverbed. They are comfortable to use in cold conditions and you can also use them as the mast and gaff of a sailing rig.

A single length of aluminium makes for a great working tool for serious poling. There is a need for flex but not too much. It can be cut to a length of 3.3–3.5m. The addition of a spike gives a better grip on the riverbed. Competition polers often mark the pole into sections with electrical tape so that there is a middle colour and then two other sections to each end mirroring each other in colour. This way, they can easily tell how close to an end they are in the heat of competition.

There are two main schools of thought on **stance and balance**. Many advocate a diagonal stance where the feet are wide and diagonal across the canoe. However, some of us have moved over to the style of the competition poler with a square stance, where the feet are wide and square across the canoe. When moving a heavily laden canoe or working as a fishing guide and poling a customer, a flat boat and diagonal stance work. I use a diagonal stance on occasion but, for the vast majority of time, and certainly when it gets hard, I will be square. The square stance enables you to use edging to steer the canoe.

Single-piece aluminium poles are awkward to transport. They can be bent into the curve of the canoe but do not store them this way or they will take on a permanent bend.

This is a little challenge for testing your balance and the stability of your canoe on its edge. The pole is resting on the water. For the less bold, do it in shallow water and use the bottom.

Getting used to edging is key. The feet are spread across the canoe and you pump the weight from one foot to the other. The body remains upright and it is merely the swift transfer of weight from foot to foot. Stability will vary from canoe to canoe.

Another useful exercise involves using the pole to provide a low brace either to the water or, if you are cautious, to the riverbed; weight is then transferred to the right foot. The left toes are still in contact and are ready to push down and flatten the canoe. The body is upright with the weight above the right foot and inside the canoe.

Paddling with the pole saves you the trouble of changing from pole to paddle and back again when you come across a short deep section. The pole is very efficient when used like a kayak paddle; swift strokes on either side enable you to get up a fair speed. This a good exercise for balance, and is a useful technique. Grip the pole the same way as you would a kayak paddle. The canoe is bow light.

An outside pivot turn with the pole: a cross-deck bow draw is followed by a sweep. Hands are at the end of the pole.

Poling off the bottom is crucial; this is how you propel your canoe upstream.

The canoe is moving so the pole is dropped into the water alongside. Both hands have the thumbs on the top for a power grip. With the pole angled, you can push the canoe forwards. (If it is too vertical, you will lift yourself rather than push the canoe.) With the pole at 45 degrees you can put effort into the push. In easy situations the arms and body rotation do the work. When power is needed, use your full weight by flexing the knees and dropping the body. Once your body has rotated and the pole is at the end of the useful thrust, the canoe has forward speed. The pole is recovered and will go back to vertical ready to drop in again.

The canoe is entering the current and starting a turn to the left. The cross-bow rudder is tightening the turn.

An important aspect of poling technique is the ability to **swap sides** at speed. At the end of the push you reach back with the rear hand and turn it so your hand points down the pole. The left hand lifts the pole beginning to swing the forward end of the pole to the opposite side of the canoe. The right hand will swap directions as the pole swings across. In the final photo of the sequence, both thumbs are up and in the power grip position.

With a good plant with the pole you can go **hand over hand** to the top. In the photo the canoeist has done this and is now preparing for one good dynamic thrust to carry him up and over to the easier water.

For me, turning using edge is a fundamental part of the square style of poling. To turn left, put your weight onto your right foot. The left foot is used to balance the canoe and is ready to push down if necessary. The pole is wide of the stern, running back at about 45 degrees. With weight on the right foot, pull in with the back hand and push out and across with the top hand. The canoe turns to its left. If you wished to turn back, you would swap sides and do the opposite. (The water is powerful in the sequence below, so the paddler has to commit to the edge and pole. At the height of the turn, the body is dynamic with considerable force bending the pole.)

The incomparable Harry Rock climbing a ledge. Photo courtesy of Harry Rock.

At the final stage, throw the pole forwards through your hands ready for the next plant. Pulling the back of the canoe to the pole does the straightening up. The pole may stay fixed to the riverbed or it may slide.

Moving upriver we need to read the water. **Eddies** allow a rest and easier progress. To move on, gather speed working up the eddy. When crossing the eddy line, anticipate the canoe trying to turn right by throwing the pole to your right and edging to the right. With all of the weight on your right foot, use a powerful thrust to send the canoe upstream and straighten it to the current. When the canoe is facing upstream, begin to flatten it.

It can be hard to coordinate this, so finding a relatively shallow area allows someone to hold your boat as you get set up. Shallower water is helpful.

Eddies allow a rest.

If you want some real fun, try **tandem poling** with two of you standing in the boat. Talk to each other! Some will pole with the stern standing and the bow kneeling and using a paddle. Be gentle.

Snubbing

When travelling downstream you will generally be driving the boat forwards, so use the same techniques as going upstream. Snubbing is a way of slowing the boat down and controlling its speed while going downstream in shallow water. You may occasionally want to slow the canoe while travelling downstream. You can even use a series of reverse ferries with the pole. In the days of birch bark canoes, snubbing protected the bow in shallow rapids.

The canoe is stern light so the upstream current does not grab the stern and turn the boat. My feet are square across the canoe. I keep the pole stretched out in front of me and at as low an angle as reasonable. If I am slowing the boat, I will jab at the bottom rather than try to stop dead. When the pole is planted, I can move the bow to and from the pole.

When the pole is in front of you it is best not to cross the body; if it jammed you would be swept from the canoe. Swap from side to side by throwing the pole over your head.

If you want to quickly move sideways then you can plant the pole at right angles and do a quick shove. The pole is unlikely to jam but, if it does, your exit will be quick.

There are only two types of poler: those of us that have swum, and those of you that are going to.

Swims & Rescues

... now you don't!

(Lena is wearing a BA under her jacket.)

> *The line was wrong. I could not correct the angle and the diagonal wave threw us left towards the main rapid. A massive area of folds and boils sucked us down. It was a deep long 'swim'; I was first in a very dark place and then the light turned to green. The surface did not get any closer for all my effort. I remember thinking I needed to buy a bigger buoyancy aid. Eventually I came up for a gulp of air before another, but briefer, down time. This next time I was up for good, but I was out of air and energy and frankly quite freaked. It took a minute or so of air and calming before I could look around me and assess the situation.*

Steve was running down the right shore and the canoe was against the rocks. Lina was out and safe on the left shore. I swam right and, as soon as I could get my breath, set off up the bank to assist Steve. By the time I got there the canoe was gone – it had re-circulated up the eddy and back into the main rapid. The canoe had swung into the massive eddy river left below the rapid, and was gently turning in the centre of this. The situation was stable.

Steve and Mike were going to paddle back upstream from above the rapid and then cross to river left before portaging. This was going to take a long time so I made the decision to swim the river to the left bank. It was flat and relatively slow. I could do that safely and then judge if I could swim out for the canoe in this relatively gentle eddy.

The swim was slow but no problem. Having made it to the other side, I then came back up the bank to the eddy. Another swim reconnected me with the canoe. I found it impossible to flip the canoe upright until I attached a tape and went to the other side to pull it over.

I remounted and paddled ashore, chastised and rueing my miss on the line. No gear was damaged or lost; only my pride had taken a hammering. Once we were sorted Lina, bless her, offered to give the rapid another go. My 'no' was emphatic! **"**

The danger of the swamped canoe.

When you take a Swim

All of a sudden you, paddles and canoe are all heading downstream. The canoe, swamped and heavy with water, is a hazard. You have to make a decision whether to stick with it or get clear. If you stay with the canoe, you must be upstream of it. The stern paddler has got the swim line and is going to attempt to swim that ashore[1]. The bow paddler has grabbed his paddle and is about to swim clear.

You could hit a rock and the canoe be swept onto you. The canoe can fold, pinning you with incredible force. The force would be catastrophic and, in these situations, limbs have been snapped. In some cases the canoe had to be sawn in two to free the person.

When swimming in rapids keep your wits about you. Do not be a victim. You can swim defensively while being carried downstream: feet should be on the surface and pointing downstream[2]. Arms are used to keep yourself pointing downstream, or even to set an angle and reverse ferry glide. If there is an unavoidable rock, you can use your feet to fend it off. Save your energy until safety is within sprinting distance or you need to swim hard to avoid a hazard.

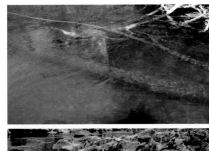

You can only swim fast for short bursts, so timing is crucial. Stay on your back in shallow water to avoid foot entrapments. In deep water, turn onto your front for a serious swimming effort. Do not let the feet drop down and sprint for that eddy![3]

There may be logs or roots or cracks in the rocks, and in flood there will be speed and power. It is vital to keep your feet on the surface. If your feet get caught then you are likely to be folded over and at risk of being pushed underwater. This is known as a ***foot entrapment***. If in doubt, swim on your back with your feet and hands on the surface.

In high water, all of these pits, potholes and cracks will be covered.

Principles of Rescue

For a specialist book on the subject see *Whitewater Safety and Rescue* by Franco Ferrero.

Any approach to safety and rescue should be informed by the following basic principles. The main thing is that anybody in a tricky situation should try to get themselves out of trouble, and not rely on being rescued.

Self, team, victim, equipment. In terms of safety we follow a hierarchy: look after your own safety first; the team next; victim third; and then way down the list come any equipment, bags and canoes. Do not endanger life by trying to retrieve equipment.

Lower risk to higher risk. Move from lower risk to higher risk rescues only when absolutely necessary. Choose the form of rescue that is likely to succeed and involves the lowest risk. If it is obvious that it won't work, or if you try and discover that it won't work, move on to the next level.

Shout, reach, throw, row, go. This reminds us of the order of the types of rescue that are possible, from low to high risk

From lower to higher risk.

Shout or point. The swimmer may need some direction from the 'rescuer', e.g. 'swim this way' or 'go that way'. Indeed, if we rescue the inexperienced needlessly, then they never build up the skills to rescue themselves.

Reach. From the bank you can reach out to the swimmer with a paddle, pole or even canoe. Do not get pulled in when an enthusiastic swimmer grabs your offering.

Throw. You can use a throw bag or other rope to reach your swimmer and pull them out. There is a definite risk in using ropes in whitewater, however, and people have drowned after being tangled in a throw rope that snagged.

Row. Often you are in your canoe when dealing with a capsize. Approach a swimmer with care and give clear orders. Getting the swimmer to kick, and even swim with one hand, can give you an extra acceleration to cross an eddy line.

Go. Entering the water as a rescuer to assist a victim is a last resort. It will put the rescuer at a heightened risk. It has to be done on occasion, particularly if the victim is unconscious or cannot be expected to grab a line, but if using rescue harnesses it is recommended that you attend a specialist course.

A short piece of rope or tape hanging from the stern makes it easier for a swimmer to grab hold without tipping you. They must not wrap it around their hand. The ability to let go is crucial.

❚❚ *I was paddling with Martin Dutton on the Tryweryn, a river that we had usually paddled in kayaks. Most things went well but the river seemed to come at us far faster in a tandem canoe than in a kayak. Eventually we started down one of the more sustained rapids.*

We took on water early and swamped. We managed to stay upright with the amount of buoyancy in the air bags, but lacked manoeuvrability and were taking on more water and glancing off rocks.

We hit one more rock. I desperately braced on the left with my head low to the water. My feet came unstuck from the stern seat and I fell head-first into the rapid. I surfaced, glanced downstream only to see the canoe still upright with Martin frantically paddling away at the front.

I rolled onto my front, swam aggressively for the shore and quickly started legging it down the bank. Martin was still paddling, managing to keep the canoe upright.

As he paddled into easier water I sprinted past him. He looked across. Shock registered on his face. He glanced over his shoulder to the stern. Then he glanced back to me on the bank and once more to the empty seat in the stern. My attempts to help failed at this point. I could only sit on the grass convulsed by laughter. His double-take was priceless. **❚❚**

First Aid & Resuscitation

The size of a first aid kit will depend on where you are and the size of the group. Further afield, a small wilderness first aid book for extra information is useful.

A standard first aid kit is not always appropriate when the casualty is in paddling kit. A triangular dressing has been cut from a bivi bag and is super-sized.

Do a first aid course to learn resuscitation. Some courses are orientated towards outdoor sports or have a strong aquatic component, allowing you to train with realistic scenarios.

Swim Lines

One method of self-rescue is to use a swim line. An easy outfitting is to clip a throw line to the back of boat and place it under some shock cord on the rear deck. A screw-gate karabiner prevents it clipping to anything else by mistake.

When using a swim line the swimmer works his way to the upstream of the canoe and takes a look to plan and time his swim. He takes the end of the rope into his hand and starts his swim to the bank. Moving down the bank, the canoeist swings the canoe towards the shore. If the current is strong, he can take a turn around a tree or a branch.

Some canoeists put a swim line at both ends of the canoe and some make their own bags which are shaped to the airbag and end of the canoe. This way the canoe end still has a clean profile which is less likely to snag.

⚠ **WARNING**

Some paddlers will not use a swim line as they believe the risk of entanglement outweighs any advantages.

Simple but effective swim line set-up.

The swimmer has righted the canoe so it will pull through the water more readily. The paddle has been thrown into the canoe and the swimmer is on his front, swimming aggressively for the bank.

Throw Lines

The throw bag is a convenient way of carrying rope for a variety of rescues. The large throw bag in the photo holds 20m of highly visible 10mm floating rope, and the smaller bag contains 18m of 7.5mm rope. In general, the thicker the rope, the easier it is for both rescuer and swimmer to hold. However, many people will find the lighter bag easier to throw. In both cases, the loop at the bottom of the bag is deliberately small so that people cannot get a hand into it. It is critical to be able to let go of a rope that may be holding you underwater, so hands must not be trapped. There is no knot or handle on the opposite end of the rope to the bag, the rope is CLEAN. This really limits the chance of a hand being trapped or if the rope is pulled clear of the rescuer then it considerably less likely to snag between rocks. Ropes snagged in powerful current are a real risk to anyone in the water.

With this bag the rope is attached to a metal ring via a figure-of-eight knot. There is a good-sized tail on the knot to allow for slippage under extreme loading. This system enables you to detach the rope from the bag.

The risk of entanglement is real so a knife should be carried.

With other bags, the rope may make up the end loop and be knotted inside the bag. Check the knot which fastens the rope into the bag. This is tied with a bowline, but the tail is woefully inadequate[1].

Twenty metre throw bag and rope.

A ***swimmer rescue using a throw line*** is shown in the above sequence. The rescuer shouts 'Rope!' to the swimmer and gets his attention. Holding the throw bag up gives a visual signal so that the swimmer knows the rope is coming. The rope is thrown across the swimmer which sends any excess rope clear.

The swimmer grabs the rope and must not take a loop around his hand, as he may need to let go. The rescuer's hands are on the rope with the thumbs up and he drops into a crouch to take the strain. The pull may bring him back upright. If the pull is too great, he can twist his hands back and allow the rope to run freely to remove the strain. He would then drop his weight and re-grip the rope as previously. The swimmer swings into the bank and the rescuer can move down the rope to assist him. Most importantly, the thrower has planned where to swing the swimmer.

Taking the throw bags on an inspection covers two possibilities: someone could slip into the water while inspecting and it may be decided to place a thrower at the end of the section.

Dry land practice. We started with static shots to practise throwing, then progressed onto moving targets and finally while holding the rope.

The swimmer has the rope over one shoulder and is holding it on his chest. If you are the swimmer take responsibility for yourself. If the thrower is about to swing you to a dangerous place, ignore the rope and swim.

On clear banks you can take a more dynamic approach. Having bagged the swimmer, you keep the strain off by running down the banks to keep level with him. By running inland and pulling the rope through your hands, you can get swimmer, boat and paddle to the bank.

If the bank is poor for standing, then the rope holder can run it around their waist. Someone can back the rescuer up by holding onto the belayer (rope holder). The belayer faces the direction of pull. The force is much greater and the swimmer can disappear below the surface. The belayer can let out some rope to relieve the strain on the swimmer.

On repacking, the rope should be stuffed back in a little at a time. When stuffed from the bag end first, it runs out easily when thrown. Running the rope over one shoulder or through a karabiner on the buoyancy assists with the packing. The karabiner should not be left in this position, as it could be a snag hazard.

Towing the empty canoe to the side.

Recovering the Canoe

The swimmer must be the priority but, once they are ashore, you can recover the canoe. If recovering the canoe would be risky at this point wait until it floats down to a safer location for retrieval.

The rescuer is doing a curl rescue as on flat water. Grasping the capsized canoe before standing, everything is stable. As she throws the righted canoe down, she drops her weight to retain stability.

Some will do a curl while still kneeling.

You can either push, shove or tow the emptied canoe to the bank. Rescuing a fully loaded canoe then towing will be an option. Turn it upright as it will travel easier through the water. When towing on moving water, avoid the quick-release knots we use on flat water: they are not quick enough. A turn around a thwart and a knee on the end of the rope is safer. In the worst case of the towed boat becoming jammed, the rope will come free without effort.

When the water has power, the canoe can pin on an obstruction and you may need to find a way of **pulling boats off**. Before getting a rope attached, you should consider the direction of pull. Work with the water rather than against it. A high pull point may assist by lifting an end clear of the water. Consider the safety of other paddlers who may be endangered by ropes strung across a river; put someone upstream to warn others.

This boat had been abandoned. It is a hired sit-on-top, known by many as a 'rent-a-crash'. The pull had to be from the far bank. The simplest way of increasing the power is to use lots of people.

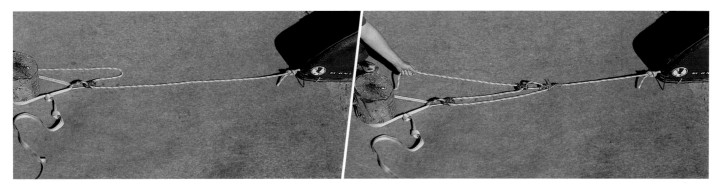

When a straight pull is not sufficient, then we resort to pulley systems for a mechanical advantage. A simple system that gives good mechanical advantage is known as a **Z drag**.

The rope is run from the canoe to a sling attached to a good anchor; this may be a tree or large boulder. Judgement is required in the selection of anchors as the forces applied are huge.

A prusik loop is attached to use as a friction hitch, in this case a French prusik (middle right), and the main rope is looped back and through a second pulley. You could attach directly to the canoe if it was in reach or via a knot in the position of the prusik loop. The prusik loop enables you to reposition the attachment.

A second French prusik is added at the left-hand pulley. This prusik is on the rope coming directly from the canoe and is being used as an auto block or clutch. The rope will travel freely through the prusik when you pull, but the rope cannot return. This allows the right-hand prusik to be reset (lower right).

If the Z drag is very close to the bank, the pull can continue all the way to the shore. There are however many occasions where the canoe, once free, will be in the main current, and it may be necessary to lower it to the best landing spot. This is difficult with a Z drag which only works effectively as a pull; a **pig rig** solves this problem.

The red rope runs from the end of the canoe and around the tree. This rope needs to be held by a second person. The pulley system is piggy-backed onto the red rope using the yellow rope.

A prusik is put onto the red rope and a pulley attached. The rope near the throw bag is run through this pulley. The yellow rope then runs back to the tree and through a karabiner: do not use a pulley here as the rope does not move during the pull but only when the whole system is being repositioned for a second pull. The rope now runs to a pulley attached to the bottom of the bag and through that. It then goes back to the pullers. This gives a 4:1 system that is easy to adjust. Each time the yellow is pulled in, the slack on the red rope is taken up. The boat is held on the red rope when the pulley system is being readjusted.

Once the boat is pulled clear of the obstruction, it can be held on the red rope. This allows you to strip the pulley gear and, using the red rope, lower the canoe further down the river to a convenient recovery spot.

The person in blue is anchoring the boat, while the person standing in the water repositions the pig rig for a second pull. When the canoe eventually came clear, it was flooded and still in a considerable force of water. It was held on the rope that ran around the tree and the pulley system was detached. It was then lowered and swung to the bank.

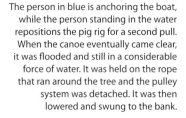

The sequence above shows a **vector pull** in use. The rope running from the canoe to the tree has been tensioned using a pig rig, but this was not enough to pull the boat off. It has been fastened off and the pig rig dismantled. A second rope has been fastened, by a sliding karabiner, at right angles to the first.

A pull is applied to the second rope. This bends the first rope multiplying the force applied. The force can in fact be close to the breaking strength of the first rope. In the final photo, the vectored pull is about to bring the canoe off.

3 metres of tape and a folding knife are carried in the buoyancy aid

According to the grade of water and the situation, it may be advisable to carry a bigger rescue kit. Many of us wear a bum bag to carry this. Two pulleys, prusik loops, extra sling, saw and waterproof wound dressing all fit into the bum bag. In a wilderness setting, I may fit in a basic survival kit.

The tape is turned into a sling with an overhand knot. Long tails are essential. Some people advise a second overhand in the tails. If massive force is applied to the sling, a single overhand knot can start moving along the tails and release itself.

When unable to get a canoe off by pulling from the ends, try a **_roll over._** The photo sequence shows the method; in reality it could be pulled off easily.

The rescuer has accessed the boat from below. It could be by canoe or swimming, but not from above; this avoids ending up under the pinned canoe or being caught in loose rope.

Pulls from the end have 'failed'. The rope from the canoe to the far bank is still in place. The rescuer is tying a 3m length of tape to the mid-thwart[1] (it could be rope). The loop around the thwart is being tied big enough that it can eventually be slid down to the submerged gunwale. Keeping the knot at the top, he feeds the other end of the tape into the water upstream of the canoe. There will be water going under the canoe that can suck the tape through[2]. With the tape through, he lets the knot slide down into the water and to the submerged gunwale. A throw bag is thrown and attached to the tape[3].

Everything is set up and the rescuer is clear[4]. The roll-over team may need considerable force on their rope and can use a pulley system to get the canoe moving[5]. Once the roll over begins, speed will be crucial and it may be best to grab the rope and heave. At the critical moment, when the canoe is upright and clear of the rock, the end pullers heave it clear[6]. Any hesitation and it will be back in place. As soon as the roll is completed, the roll-over team slackens off. The boat is flooded and in strong current, so the end rope team use a tree as a friction brake.

In a real situation even getting the tape in position is hard. Nobody must be above the canoe because of the danger of being swept under it. Even although it does not do a full roll, it is enough to free the canoe and the end pullers heave it clear. With some judicious kicking and bending, the canoe could be paddled.

Early morning brew on the Mississagi.

Canoe Country

▌▌ *Well so much for the Wilderness! For months Lina had spoken of little else in relation to the trip. No mention of the river or lake; It was all about her first floatplane trip.*

The outfitter dropped us off at the floatplane base on Red Lake for our pending flight to Artery Lake. Bad news awaited us: the cloud base was far too low to fly as the 55 mile flight had to cross a ridge. In the spare time suddenly available, we got sorted and weighed both the gear and ourselves in readiness for any clearance.

Late in the day we were in with a chance and so our spirits lifted, but we could not cross the ridge. Our pilot was much younger than the Norseman he was flying (not unusual with these northern flying workhorses). Our only chance of getting out that day was to follow the circuit of lakes that swung around the ridge. It was a bit hit-or-miss, and if the cloud dropped we would have to turn back.

The take-off was the usual floatplane smooth transition from water to sky. Soon the novelty wore off for Lina and the incessant rhythmic droning of the aircraft had her asleep with her head on my shoulder in minutes. So much for the excitement! We flew just below the clouds through the occasional curtain of rain. Both the pilot and myself were following the route on our maps.

Lina woke up before we landed and watched in wonder and amazement. We arrived over Artery Lake, and a quick fly-through located a possible campsite and checked out the landing area for obstructions. Within minutes we were ashore and unloading; the pilot wanted out of there quickly before the weather closed down.

The Norseman taxied away down the lake. The sound of high revs accompanied the plane as it came back in view while lifting into the air. Shortly after, it returned for one last fly-by and then was gone. Only an hour before we had left the small town of Red Lake and now we were in the wilderness. I looked around at the others. They stood in silence suddenly aware that we were totally alone and committed to the journey ahead. **"**

'Canoe country' speaks to me of wild or semi-wild country such as is found in North America, Scandinavia or even to a degree in parts of Scotland, where you are totally dependent on your canoe as a means of transport and your outdoor skills for shelter, warmth and food. The further you are into a wilderness the more serious any incident will be. Poor planning, the loss of a boat, a cut from the careless use of axe or knife, a broken bone or general illness will have far greater consequences. Caution and care should be our watchwords in this environment.

Planning a Wilderness Trip

The further we are from help the more self-reliant we must be. Careful planning and preparation are essential.

Guidebooks will vary considerably in detail. While on a 360-mile trip which included the Bonnet Plume River in the NW of Canada, our guidebook provided a page and a half of information. It gave details of the major rapids and their location but left the majority of the decision-making to the paddlers. At the other end of the spectrum is Hap Wilson's guide to the Missinaibi: a whole book to describe one river. In Hap's book every rapid has a detailed map with information on its lines and problems. A lot of environmental and historical detail was also included. Both treatments have their advantages but you have to be aware that things can change; trees can block a rapid and higher water will increase the difficulty. On a trip on the Bloodvein in Manitoba the water levels went ballistic; grade 2 rapids became massive grade 4s and portages became longer and harder.

Left: compass orientates the map to north.
Centre: compass used to paddle on a bearing.

On trips we need **maps** as well as guide books. The map is housed in a waterproof case. On this trip the guidebook information has been transferred to the map.

In darkness or mist or perhaps on a very large lake a compass is vital. We can paddle on a bearing in poor visibility, or to work out the angle of a section of river or shoreline to help place us. We can use it to orientate the map (by aligning north of the map with the north of the compass), making it easier to work out places and directions.

▐▐ *In the late 1980s I organised a kayak trip down the Grand Canyon of the Colorado. I sent for information by letter, waited for stuff to go back and forth across the Atlantic, responded to it and then eventually arranged the last details by a very expensive phone call. It didn't help that the outfitter had the slowest Midwest drawl that I had come across and I spent minutes willing him to get through a sentence. Fortunately, credit cards were available so I didn't have to carry wads of cash or travellers cheques when I eventually met the outfitter.* **▐▐**

Outfitters are now to be found in many parts of the world. This makes life much easier as it is possible to hire canoes and source all your needs locally. In North America, decide where you want to paddle and then put the name of the area or river plus the word outfitter into an Internet search engine. This will get you details of the various outfitters and the services they provide. This is what they do for a living and the service tends to be good. They can arrange for canoe hire, permits, fishing licences, cooking gear, food and even camping gear if you want. Typically, they also arrange shuttles or even book floatplane flights if the trip starts with a fly in. If it is a flat-water area, then take the option of hiring a lightweight Kevlar canoe. Portages are easier and paddling is a delight. On the steeper river of the Canadian west, it is possible to hire canoes with full spray covers that are necessary in the bigger volume and waves.

It may be worth putting a brief résumé of the rivers you have done and the experience you have. This will make it easier for the outfitter to advise you. Contact can be by email and VoIP (Voice over inter protocol e.g. Skype).

Scandinavia has similar services, although the canoe designs tend to be a bit basic and designed for beginners on flat water.

In England and Wales, gear hire tends to be for very easy rivers like the Wye. Scotland has a number of outfitters who can arrange boats and shuttles.

Communications

The world and its wilderness has become a smaller place. Until relatively recently, once you paddled off you were on your own. Any accident or delay, and you had to sort it out unaided. Most of us now don't think twice about carrying a mobile phone in more accessible places, but these will not work in the remote areas of the world.

Relatively simple accidents can, in a remote setting, prove fatal so the ability to alert the outside world in an emergency could be a lifesaver. One solution is to carry a **satellite phone**. Few of us will own one but they are easy to hire from online companies. In North America many canoe outfitters will rent them to you. Normally there is a per-day charge plus a deposit for any calls made. They are expensive to use but because of the two-way nature of the call, rearrangements of shuttles, emergency aid or even the ability to talk directly to a doctor make them very versatile. These phones are now a reasonable size and weight. Because they communicate via satellites it is possible to call from almost anywhere, but they will not work in deep canyons or even under dense tree cover.

EPIRBs (emergency position-indicating radio beacons) have long been in use with sailors operating offshore. These have not proved popular with land-based adventurers, however. Now there is a recommended alternative with a **PLB** (personal locator beacon) that is for personal use and intended to indicate a person in distress who is away from a normal telephone emergency service. They are so effective that, in Australia, some National Parks have issued them to hikers.

PLBs also rely on satellites. They are about the price of a top-quality buoyancy aid, plus an annual subscription that is only slightly less. The best models have a range of responses. They can allow others to track your progress and even show your GPS location on an online map; an OK button allows you to send a pre-programmed message along with your GPS position to selected contacts; a Help button notifies others that you need assistance that is non-life threatening; and, finally, a SOS button can alert others to a critical emergency. Both the Help and SOS buttons should have a protective cover to prevent accidental alerts.

The one certainty is that technology will move on quickly. This makes the above advice very time sensitive, so keep an eye on developments.

A Spot Messenger: an example of a Personal Location Beacon.

Baker Tent, photo courtesy of Ray Mears.

Living in Canoe Country

The canoe fits into the landscape so perfectly you would be forgiven for thinking it was designed by Mother Nature herself. As adventurers and visitors to such landscapes, we should aim to fit into it with the same perfection and integrity. We are only the brief custodians of these environments; it is essential that the utmost respect and care is taken if they are to survive for future generations. We need to learn how to live in those surroundings rather than merely exist. Our kit will have a profound impact on our experience.

The right choice of kit is important for comfort in the environment we travel in. You may want a large *tent* to provide a base while, at other times, the length of trip and portages will dictate the need to go small and light.

The Baker Tent is a modern version of the classic campfire tent made famous by the late great canoeist, artist and filmmaker, Bill Mason. This traditional design features a wide front opening with a large overhead canopy, enabling you to enjoy your surroundings to the full while warmed by the fire and sheltered from the elements above. In poor weather, the side panels can be fastened across the front of the tent. For Bill this seemed to be an ideal solution when filming or painting in the same spot for a period; however, it is very heavy for those on the move.

In some locations we will need a degree of ingenuity. Free-standing tents that do not depend on pegs may be best in areas where the only clear ground tends to be sand or rocky. Mosquito nets are a necessity wherever there are mozzies, midges or the myriad of other bugs sent to torment. In bug season, care is needed when entering the tent. Turning the torches off just before getting in at night seems to attract less bugs.

A most un-wilderness campsite. Sometimes you just have to take the only possibility. We had pitched camp in the early hours of the morning on the first available spot along the Shropshire Union Canal after the city of Chester. Arwel had spent the night worrying about rolling into the water and the local kids heading to school woke all of us.

Tarps (see next page) make for a great shelter on trips; sleeping under a tarp allows us to be part of the environment in a way that a tent does not. In poor weather, they provide an agreeable social area as long as the mosquitoes or flies are not too bad. In such conditions you can use tents as bedrooms and the tarp as a living area. It makes for a greater group harmony, as folk can sit and chat. Kit can be dried rather than left damp in the corner of a tent. When putting them up, it helps if you have plenty of cord and a touch of imagination.

On the Bloodvein we had decided not to take stoves. The tarp sheltered the fire or we would never have managed to cook in the poor weather. Being on rock, we used a tripod to hang the pots.

A lean-to on the banks of the Bonnet Plume. A central hang point stops the middle being blown towards the working area. Attachment points allow for versatility in creating a shelter. Photo courtesy of Tony Howard.

The Missinaibi after a thunderstorm. The forest had suffered a fire some years before and the undergrowth was so dense that we were camped on the shore. An A-frame was constructed using driftwood and the tarp hung from it. The edges were fastened to the canoes and rocks were used to guy the whole thing out. We weighted the canoes to stop them being blown around.

Cliff Jacobson is often credited with inventing the Tundra Tarp for the far North of Canada, where the flies and mosquitoes can be horrendous. Netting hangs from the sides give respite from the small beasties. Photo courtesy of Paul Fulbrook.

For convenience, the front of the tent had been put under the tarp.

Good company and a blazing fire.

A small firebox needs dry wood so, in wet weather, wood will need to be cut and split to get at its dry heart. Larger fireboxes work well.

Bacon and pancakes. By raking embers from the active fire under the grill, temperature can be controlled to a degree.

Fires and Cooking

The wood was dead and the fire was built on sand. The embers and ash were cleaned away the next morning. In some areas of North America, it is a requirement to use a fire tray to prevent the ash mixing with the sand. Any large pieces of charcoal are either taken with you and relit the next day or treated as waste and carried out; it is normally advocated that the fine ash is disposed of in the river. Some areas are being trashed by people using wood fires, so care is needed in the choice of site and wood.

Generally I carry either a small gas stove on a short trip or a liquid fuel stove on longer ones. Stoves can be an issue when flying with commercial airlines. Gas cylinders are out for safety reasons but security people have a dislike of any liquid fuel stove, regularly confiscating those that have a fuel tank. Even washing the fuel tank out with soapy water beforehand does not seem to appease them. Flying with an axe or a knife in hold luggage does not seem to be an issue, however.

Some people use Dutch ovens for baking on a trip but they are heavy. A modern lightweight alternative is this Outback Oven. Sitting on the gas stove is a heat spreader to prevent a burn spot in the pan. The pan has a lid and, to the left, a cover to go over everything. The cover spreads the heat all around the pot. Pizzas, cakes and bread can be baked.

A tripod is formed with the tie being a thin green stick that has been twisted to form a flexible withy. This is knotted around the tripod with a section dangling below. A fork has been left at the foot of the withy to hang the pot. The same can be achieved using a length of light chain with a hook at the end. If you want the pot higher, you bring the legs of the tripod inwards. The fire in the photo is on bare rock.

Another effective method is to use a sloped arm and a separate pot hanger. The hanger has been notched with a series of downward points. The sloping branch has been trimmed at the end and a small hole left for the points of the pot hanger. This is a very adjustable and elegant method.

Knife and axe can be used to create feather sticks for fire lighting, rather than carrying firelighters.

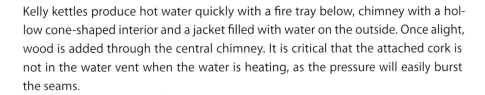

Kelly kettles produce hot water quickly with a fire tray below, chimney with a hollow cone-shaped interior and a jacket filled with water on the outside. Once alight, wood is added through the central chimney. It is critical that the attached cork is not in the water vent when the water is heating, as the pressure will easily burst the seams.

The fire risk can be horrendous with the forest one giant area of tinder. A cigarette end or someone burning toilet paper started this[1]. It quickly spread and ate its way into rotten logs and tree stumps. This one was stopped with a desperate effort. Wet towels were used to beat the flames and water was carried to the site. Logs had to be split open to check for the fire smouldering away.

A fire should be on sand, damp soil or rock if possible, but not tree mould. Do not burn a forest down. At times you are better off not lighting a fire. In many countries there are total fire bans at the driest times of the summer, so don't head for the wilds of Canada in August believing you are going to be cooking on wood fires.

Finishing a bannock (traditional unleavened bead) by turning it towards the fire. It will be eaten for the next day's lunch along with a selection of jam, cheese and treats.

❶

Fishing is a great way to supplement the diet on a long trip. Most places, wilderness or not, will require a licence or permit. Photo courtesy of Mike Hazelhurst.

I recommend the book *How to Shit in the Woods* by Kathleen Meyer ISBN 978-1580083638. It tells you far more than is suggested by the title.

Water is the most basic commodity, but in many places water will need to be purified. There are lots of methods but here we are using a filter pump. On longer trips I use either a pump or boil some water on the fire. Various chemical treatments are readily available, but read the instructions carefully in every case. For example, iodine (which is very effective) should not be used for more than a few weeks each season; it can cause thyroid problems with prolonged use.

Disposing of Waste

Wilderness areas are precious and the impact we have on them must be kept to a minimum. A conscious judgment must therefore be made on our own presence and any waste. I have walked into the forest from a number of well-used wilderness campsites only to find it (to my disgust) encircled by piles of human excreta decorated with bunched up toilet paper. This is totally unacceptable, leaving me to wonder if I am really sharing these places with like-minded people.

In some heavily used North American national parks, each wilderness campsite will have a simple privy toilet installed. This is a necessary strategy employed to eliminate the situation described above. In more remote places, it comes down to us to be responsible and to follow local recommendations. On a desert river it may be a requirement to pack out all solid human waste as the soil is too poor to break excreta down. In woodland areas, a small hole some 20cm deep can be dug and the material buried. Toilet paper should be buried at the bottom of the hole, burnt in the campfire or packed out. These burials should be a minimum of 60m from any water source. Female hygiene products should not be buried and should be packed out or disposed of on a campfire. Recommendation and regulations will vary from place to place and there are many variations.

Cans, glass and plastics should be packed out. In fact, some North American parks do not allow cans or glass to be taken on a trip. It's simple: if you packed it in then you pack it out.

Washing yourself or dishes should be done with a minimum of biodegradable soap and the grey water disposed of the same 60m from water sources.

Portaging

Portaging is very much part of canoe culture. The ability to portage the canoe across the Canadian Shield made it such a versatile journeying tool. To this day, portaging is a vital element in this most evocative of canoe landscapes.

"You meet a better class of person once past the first portage. Because of the work involved, they are probably going to be like-minded people." Anon

On a river the start of a portage may be difficult to find or even very close to the waterfall or rapid you are going to walk around. In swift water it is best to be cautious and pull in early. Judge the water levels; in high water show far more caution. There may be a sign to indicate the start of the trail. In the days of the Voyageurs, a pine tree could be ring barked and its branches stripped to provide a marker at the portage start. Finding the next portage on a lake may require detailed navigation. In North America, guidebooks will give details but elsewhere river guides are generally written for kayaks and will you need to make your own decisions.

Take kit across the portage first, then you know what the track is going to be like with the canoe. Many portage trails are maintained in North America, but there may be new trees down. Many will double bag the carry: one heavy sack and a second on top, packed with the light but bulky items. Paddles are best strapped together to make one bundle. Be organised: it is so easy to put something down and lose it.

In a wilderness situation, whether at the start or end of a portage or leaving a campsite, it is best that the last person does a 'paranoia check'. Assume that you have left something and have a good last look around. It will save losing that vital piece of gear.

The going is not always easy. Portage in pairs: the 'spare' person acts as the eyes of the carrier and prevents them walking into anything. It is easy to swap over on long portages. The carrier stops and slopes the stern of the canoe to the ground. The other person comes under the front and holds the canoe up with straight arms. The carrier can then step out from under and take over holding the front up. The other then steps under the yoke and the portage continues. Know when to double up to carry: both you and the canoe need protecting. In a wilderness environment a heavy fall on bad ground with a weighty canoe could be a serious matter.

In Temagami Jamie is portaging a Kevlar canoe; the trip was on lakes so we had no need of a heavy whitewater boat. The portaging was a pleasure.

Bears and Other Beasties

There is an apparent calm and profound beauty to be found in any wilderness; however, you will be sharing this with many others, both minute and massive. Some of these encounters will enhance your experience, whether the presence of the majestic stag or soaring eagle in Scotland (and maybe soon the shy beaver) or the magnificent moose, bear, beaver and otters in Canada (all of which are backed by the wailing lament of the loon). Some of the experiences we share are downright unpleasant, but even the experiences which we do want to encounter have their issues. Preparation and understanding is therefore paramount in order to limit the discomfort and problems you can be faced with when travelling in and sharing this wonderful environment.

Midges are bad enough, but mosquitoes can be a torment. In the middle photo[1] the horizontal welt is from a long portage with wet boots. On a hot muggy evening I was encased in bug-proof clothing; this paddler was not. After-bite remedies and anti-histamine are worth carrying to reduce the itching.

Lina's eyelid has become swollen from just one bite[2]. If you know you react badly to bites, then extra care should be taken. Many women who wilderness travel carry a Shewee so they do not have to drop their trousers in mosquito-infested areas. The company that manufacture them say that the Shewee 'is a moulded plastic funnel that provides women with a simple, private and hygienic method of urinating without removing clothes'. Enough said. Some carry a bug net which can be used as a portable latrine tent.

Bug repellents come in many forms. Citronella, one the many natural products available, is reasonably effective. Others are based on a solution of Deet; this is a fairly harsh chemical and is not advised for use with young children. I have tried all sorts of 'bug dope'; while most give some protection, when the bugs get really bad nothing stops them.

Keeping the bugs at bay

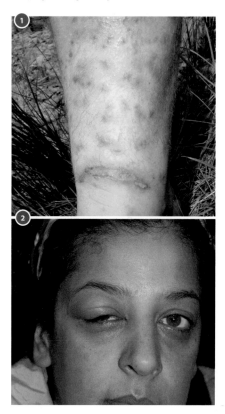

In the UK midge nets are readily available to go over just the head. In Canada I have a bug suit for bad conditions. The trousers have cuffs that fit into the boots to protect the top of the ankles. The mesh on the hood is zippered so that you can still eat. Check for the times when the flies are at their worst because there are definite seasons.

Other beasts are a bit bigger. I have yet to have a bad encounter with a bear, but I have always followed local and expert advice. Food is never stored in the campsite and, when possible, it is hauled up to hang from a branch at night. Avoid smelly food unless it can be vacuum packed and eaten in one go. Waste (in particular fish waste) is burnt or disposed of a long way from the campsite. In the more popular areas, bears can become habituated to humans and can see our packs as a food source. Some parks in North America have installed metal bear-proof storage boxes in wilderness campsites. Bear attacks on humans are fortunately extremely rare, but find out the local advice and follow it.

I have yet to paddle so far north that we are in polar bear territory. This bear is a totally different ball game, as it will actively hunt humans. Everyone I know that has travelled in such areas has taken a gun. This is well outside of my experience so seek advice.

I have carried pepper spray on some Canadian trips. The bear has got to be very close before you can direct the spray at it. Cliff Jacobson has a yarn about some German tourists who mis-read the instructions and treated it like bug spray. They duly anointed each other with pepper spray.

So far all of my own bear encounters have been trip highlights. On the Bonnet Plume, a Grizzly reared up a short distance from the river. Head raised, it sniffed at the air trying to decide what these strange canoeists were. It was the start of the trip and the river was shallow and narrow. Our strokes had a quiet deliberation in the execution. Breath was held as we sped on with the current. One corner later, we were laughing and babbling out our excitement.

Leave only footprints, just like the bear.
Photo courtesy of Tony Howard.

Pont d'Arc, River Ardèche.

In the greying light of morning and with a thin mist, we left Pont D'Arc and its improbable bridge of limestone. We slipped quietly downriver and into the mouth of the Ardèche Gorge.

Within hours this would be a crowded cacophony of paddlers in their brightly coloured plastic fleet, but for now everyone else was still tucked up asleep.

As we turned the first corner the water sped up. Lina's keen eyes spotted the first beaver tucked into a corner. As ever, I would have slid on by without noticing. At Trois Eau, in the chill of the morning, we took the easy shoot river right as we didn't want to take on water in the more fun rapid to the left. We had turned into the depths of the gorge, and the splendour of the limestone walls began to tower above us.

The mist began to burn away as we past rapid after rapid. All the lines were easy and none disturbed our quietness. I even spotted two beavers without Lina having to point them out.

The acrid smell of feral goats alerted us to their presence long before we saw them. Their nonchalance at this early morning intrusion was astounding. Light was reflecting up into the cave at Echo corner. We pulled in and Lina could not resist climbing up into its roof. A short paddle across the river took us into the sunlight and a beach of granite cobbles. It was time for breakfast: out came the coffee along with the croissants and pain au chocolat.

We paddled past the bivouac sites of Gaud and Gournier. There was only one person in sight at the latter. A raised hand in greeting and we were past and alone again. It was here that we had so often seen wild boar, but not today.

Rapids were just gentle interludes between quiet stretches of water. No playing today; the routes were chosen for speed and dryness. Even so, we were reading the river and enjoying the efficient lines.

Lina taking it easy on the Ardèche.
Canoeing can be tough.

We stopped briefly for a leg stretch. A small granite cobble, one among many others, caught my eye with its perfect roundness. It was speckled white-brown and pink, and worn smooth from its journey through the limestone gorge from the mountains many miles away.

At each bend, spectacular rock architecture rose to the rim 300m above. And at each turn we swung back and forth from shadow to full sun. The bottom of the gorge would be baking by midday, but we would be well gone by then. Black kites circled above the river.

The river made its turn towards Saint-Martin and the flat lands beyond. Finally, there was another paddler on the water. He nodded a greeting to us, the early birds. In silence we shared the companionship of the canoe and the warmth of the morning sun. **"**

Bibliography

Technique and General

Canoeing, American Canoe Association,
Human Kinetics 2008, ISBN 0736067159

Canoeing, American National Red Cross 1985, ISBN 0385083130

Canoe and Kayak Handbook, British Canoe
Union, Pesda Press 2002, ISBN 0953195657

Coaching Handbook, British Canoe Union,
Pesda Press 2006, ISBN 0954706161

Trailside Guide: Canoeing, Gordon Grant,
W.W.Norton & Co 1997, ISBN 0393314898

Thrill of the Paddle, Paul Mason and Mark Scriver,
Key Porter Books Ltd 1999, ISBN 1552630390

Path of the Paddle, Bill Mason, Key Porter
Books Ltd 1987, ISBN 0919493386

Paddle Your Own Canoe, Gary and Joanie McGuffin,
Boston Mills Press 2003, ISBN 1550463772

The Canoe Handbook, Slim Ray,
Stackpole Books 1992, ISBN 0811730328

Canoe Poling, Harry Rock,
Little Dancer Limited 2005, ISBN 0955153700

Expedition skills

Expedition Canoeing, Cliff Jacobson,
Globe Pequot Press 2005, ISBN 076273809X

Song of the Paddle, Bill Mason,
Firefly Books 1994, ISBN 1552090892

Essential Bushcraft, Ray Mears,
Hodder & Stoughton 2003, ISBN 0340829710

How to Shit in the Woods, Kathleen Meyer,
Ten Speed Press 2011, ISBN 1580083633

White Water Rescue

River Rescue, Les Bechdel and Slim Ray,
Appalachian Mountain Club 1986, ISBN 0910146551

Whitewater Safety & Rescue, Franco Ferrero,
Pesda Press 2006, ISBN 0954706153

History

Building a Birchbark Canoe, David Gidmark,
Firefly Books Ltd 2002, ISBN 155297569X

The Canoe: A Living Tradition, John Jennings,
Firefly Books Ltd 2005, ISBN 1554070805

Bark Canoes: The Art and Obsession of Tappan Adney,
John Jennings, Firefly Books Ltd 2004, ISBN 1552977331

*Canoe: History of the Craft from Panama to the
Arctic*, Kenneth Roberts and Phillip Shackleton,
Gage Distribution Co 1983, ISBN 0771595824

Northern Wilderness: Bushcraft of the Far North,
Ray Mears, Hodder & Stoughton 2010, ISBN 0340980834

Empire of the Bay, Peter C Newman,
Penguin Putnam Inc 2000, ISBN 0140299878

*Emperor of the North: Sir George Simpson and the
Remarkable Story of the Hudson's Bay Company*,
James Raffan, Harper 2010, ISBN 0062026658

*Fire in the Bones: Bill Mason and the
Canadian Canoeing Tradition*, James Raffan,
Harpercollins Canada 1997, ISBN 0006386555

DVDs

Curgenven, Justine. *This is Canoeing*
Ford, Kent, *Solo Playboating*
Mason, Bill, *Path of the Paddle*
Mason, Bill, *Song of the Paddle*
Mason, Bill, *Waterwalker*
Mears, Ray: *Bushcraft Survival Series 2* (features Ray
  Mears building a birch bark canoe and the author
  doing a wilderness journey with him)
Rock, Harry, *Canoe Poling*

Websites

www.redcanoes.ca   website of Bill Mason's family
www.songofthepaddle.co.uk   a British based canoe forum
www.canoewithaview.co.uk   a second British canoe forum
www.raygoodwin.com   the author's website
www.chrs.ca   the Canadian Heritage Rivers System
www.americancanoe.org   the American Canoe Association
www.canoemuseum.net   the amazing Canadian
  Museum with its fine collection
www.crca.ca   Paddle Canada: the national association of Canada
www.bcu.org.uk   the governing body of the sport in the UK

Index

ENDLESS RIVER

Tel: 01905 640003
www.endlessriver.co.uk

Satu Vanska-Westgarth & Luke Farrington. Soca River, Slovenia

EXPERIENCE THE LEGEND

From hidden river valleys to open lakes, Mad River Canoe has a boat to take you somewhere special. From the rugged Journey to the manoeuvrable Legend and smooth paddling Reflection, all of our designs come with a heritage of fine craftsmanship and premium quality materials.

FIND YOURS AT WWW.MADRIVERCANOE.CO.UK